LOW FAT
&
LIGHT
FOUR
INGREDIENT
COOKBOOK

By Linda Coffee and Emily Cale

Published by Coffee and Cale

ACKNOWLEDGEMENTS

Our appreciation to Marilyn Magness RD, LD, our nutrition consultant, who had the experience and patience to calculate the nutritional breakdown of each recipe.

A special thanks to all the folks at Braswell Printing; especially, Gail Gross who coordinates the production of our cookbooks - The Four Ingredient Cookbook; More of the Four Ingredient Cookbook and now, Low Fat & Light Four Ingredient Cookbook. We are glad she can keep it straight!

Thanks again to Phil Houseal for his assistance in the layout of our third cookbook!

A big thanks to the food manufacturers that are creatively supplying an ever enlarging array of fat free and low fat products for us to test and taste.

And last, to a very, very special person, Emily's mother-in-law, Wilma Cale for all her help in shopping, organizing, cooking, tasting and always being there to help us. Without her help, we would probably still be working on this book!

Special "thank you's" for their participation in cooking, testing and critiquing; their help was greatly appreciated:

1. Loma and Harold Bammel
2. Anita and Van Berson
3. Jane Maxwell and Gene Cluster
4. Chris and Dell Davis
5. Susana and Jason Dias
6. Lucy Dubuisson
7. Deda Garlitz
8. Valerie and Bill Grebe
9. Gail and Chuck Gross
10. Dawn, Hannah, Sayer, Hartley and Phil Houseal
11. Betty and Curt Johnston
12. Marilyn Magness
13. Loraine and Art Modgling
14. Patri and Brewer Newton
15. Kathy and Bill Reed
16. Mary and Rudy Rudasill
17. Virginia Stevenson

It is impossible to ignore the trend towards reducing fat in our diets. The newstands are littered with "low-fat" articles. The grocery aisles are packed with products that are fat-free, low-fat and light.

With today's hectic lifestyles, just putting a meal on the table is a major accomplishment. Now, we are supposed to put a meal on the table and reduce the fat. If this is as challenging to you, as it is to us, these simple recipes are sure to be helpful.

MARILYN SCHAD MAGNESS RD, LD

Marilyn was born in Tulsa, Oklahoma and graduated from the University of Oklahoma in Norman and then completed her Dietetic Internship at the OU Health Sciences in Oklahoma City. Following completion of the internship in 1973, she became a Registered Dietitian and worked as a Nutrition Consultant for the Dairy Council in San Antonio and Houston and as a Program Coordinator in Memphis. After having three children, Marilyn worked as a Consulting Dietitian to health care facilities and she is currently employed as a Clinical Dietitian at the South Texas Veterans Health Care System in Kerrville. She also consulted part time at Ultrafit Preventive Medicine facilities teaching nutrition and lowfat cooking classes.

The children are now teen-agers and they are learning to help with the cooking. Marilyn says, "The Four Ingredient Cookbooks are even more simple to use than some of the children's recipe books I've bought at times to encourage my children to explore cooking. My parents always encouraged me to help in the kitchen and I grew to love cooking. Like many other working parents, I just don't have time to prepare long involved recipes. I think this series of cookbooks is very timely and I am glad to be a part of the Four Ingredient Lite Cookbook."

PLEASE NOTE THE FOLLOWING ABOUT THE ANALYSIS OF THE RECIPES IN THE FOUR INGREDIENT LITE COOKBOOK:

The analysis for the cookbook was done using the Professional Nutritionist computer software program which includes the USDA database of foods and an All Foods database. Additional foods were added to the database by using manufacturer's food labels.

Recipes calling for chicken breasts were analyzed using Individually Quick Frozen (IQF) chicken breasts.

Recipes using marinades or sauces include the full amount of the ingredients listed.

Recipes may be further modified to decrease sodium by omitting salt from the recipe or by using unsalted products when available.

Recipe analysis is an approximation and different results may be obtained by using different nutrient databases. Manufacturers nutrition labels may also change from time to time.

We have listed a few helpful ingredients that are good to keep on hand in learning to cook and eat a lowfat diet!

Fat Free Margarine
Fat Free Cream Cheese
Fat Free Salad Dressings
Fat Free Sour Cream
Fat Free Ice Cream
Fat Free Yogurt
Fat Free Frozen Yogurt
Fat Free Soups
Fat Free Mayonnaise
Fat Free Lunch Meats
Fat Free Hot Dogs
Fat Free Crackers
Fat Free Sweetened Condensed Milk
Fat Free Gravies
Fat Free Flour Tortillas
Fat Free Brownies
Fat Free Cookies
Pastas in Different Shapes and Flavors
Skim Milk
Liquid Egg Substitute
Salsas
Mustard
Selection of Grains
Rice Cakes
Hot Pepper Sauce
Flavored Tomato Sauces
BBQ Sauce
Notfat Refried Beans
Flavored Vinegars
Pretzels
Fruits
Vegetables
Plain Popcorn
Dried Mushrooms
Tuna Packed in Water
Beans
Dried and Fresh Herbs and Spices

TABLE OF CONTENTS

APPETIZERS

TANGY DIP

1. 1 Cup Fat Free Sour Cream
2. 2 Tablespoons Chili Sauce
3. 2 Teaspoons Prepared Horseradish

Mix above ingredients. Cover and refrigerate at least 1 hour. Serve with fresh vegetables.

PER TABLESPOON:

Calories	8.43	Protein	1.37g
Total Fat	0g	Carbohydrates	0.80g
Saturated Fat	0g	Cholesterol	0mg
Sodium	25.85mg	Fiber	0g

CURRY DIP

1. 1 Cup Fat Free Sour Cream
2. 1 Teaspoon Curry Powder
3. 1/2 Teaspoon Lemon Juice
4. 1/2 Teaspoon Ground Cumin

Combine above ingredients and chill. Serve with fresh vegetables.

PER TABLESPOON:

Calories	8.04	Protein	1.54g
Total Fat	0.02g	Carbohydrates	0.59g
Saturated Fat	0g	Cholesterol	0mg
Sodium	7.66mg	Fiber	0.04g

CHILI CON QUESO

1. 2 Pounds Fat Free Cheddar Cheese (grated)
2. 1 Can (10 oz.) Rotel Tomatoes and Green Chilies

Melt cheese slowly in saucepan or microwave. Stir in tomatoes. Use as a dip with fat free tortilla chips.

PER TABLESPOON:

Calories	16.33	Protein	3.54g
Total Fat	0g	Carbohydrates	0.52g
Saturated Fat	0g	Cholestrol	0mg
Sodium	13.87mg	Fiber	0g

CALIFORNIA DIP

1. 2 Cups Fat Free Cottage Cheese
2. 1 Tablespoon Lemon Juice
3. 2 Tablespoons Skim Milk
4. 1 Envelope Onion Soup Mix

Mix cottage cheese and lemon juice in blender. Add skim milk. Place in bowl and stir in onion soup mix. Chill before serving with fresh vegetables.

PER TABLESPOON:

Calories	10.11	Protein	1.50g
Total Fat	0.10g	Carbohydrates	0.78g
Saturated Fat	0.04g	Cholesterol	0.59mg
Sodium	95.75mg	Fiber	0.11g

CHILE SALSA

1. 1 Cup Chopped Seeded Tomatoes
2. 1/2 Cup Chopped Green Onions
3. 1 Can (4 oz.) Diced Green Chiles

Mix above ingredients together and refrigerate. Serve with fat free tortilla chips.

PER TABLESPOON:

Calories	2.55	Protein	0.11g
Total Fat	0.02g	Carbohydrates	0.59g
Saturated Fat	0g	Cholesterol	0mg
Sodium	42.31mg	Fiber	0.17g

LIGHT GUACAMOLE

1. 1 Bag (20 oz.) Frozen Peas (defrosted)
2. 1/4 Cup Fresh Lime Juice
3. 1/2 Bunch of Green Onions (diced)
4. 1/4 Cup Picante Sauce

In blender, blend peas, lime juice and onions. Remove to mixing bowl and mix in picante sauce. Refrigerate until ready to serve. Serve with fat free tortilla chips.

PER TABLESPOON:

Calories	9.29	Protein	0.56g
Total Fat	0.03g	Carbohydrates	1.80g
Saturated Fat	0g	Cholesterol	0mg
Sodium	13.82mg	Fiber	0.62g

ALMOND FRUIT DIP

1. 2 Cups (16 oz.) Lowfat Cottage Cheese
2. 1/2 Cup Powdered Sugar
3. 1 Package (4 oz.) Fat Free Cream Cheese
4. 1 Teaspoon Almond Extract

In blender, add above ingredients and blend until smooth. Cover and chill until ready to serve. Serve with fresh fruit.

PER TABLESPOON:

Calories	16.58	Protein	1.71g
Total Fat	0.11g	Carbohydrates	2.10g
Saturated Fat	0.07g	Cholesterol	0.48mg
Sodium	57.82mg	Fiber	0g

APPLE CURRY DIP

1. 1 1/2 Cups Low Fat Cottage Cheese
2. 1 Cup Unsweetened Applesauce
3. 1 Envelope Onion Soup Mix
4. 2 Teaspoons Curry Powder

In blender, blend cottage cheese and applesauce until smooth. Stir in soup mix and curry powder. Serve with raw vegetables.

PER TABLESPOON:

Calories	11.97	Protein	1.19g
Total Fat	0.16g	Carbohydrates	1.50g
Saturated Fat	0.07g	Cholesterol	0.42mg
Sodium	122.0mg	Fiber	0.21g

ROQUEFORT DIP

1. 1/2 Cup Crumbled Roquefort or Bleu Cheese
2. 2 Cups (16 oz.) Low Fat Cottage Cheese
3. 1 Teaspoon Dried Onion Flakes
4. Pepper to taste

Combine and blend above ingredients. Chill until ready to serve. Serve with vegetables.

PER TABLESPOON:

Calories	18.67	Protein	2.02g
Total Fat	0.98g	Carbohydrates	0.37g
Saturated Fat	0.62g	Cholesterol	3.05mg
Sodium	97.32mg	Fiber	0g

SPANISH OLIVE SPREAD

1. 1 Carton (8 oz.) Fat Free Sour Cream
2. 1/4 Cup Green Pimiento Stuffed Olives (chopped)
3. 1/4 Cup Liquid From Olive Jar
4. Paprika

In blender place sour cream and olive liquid and blend until smooth. Pour into bowl and add olives. Mix thoroughly. Sprinkle with paprika and refrigerate. Serve as a spread on party rye bread.

PER TABLESPOON:

Calories	7.15	Protein	1.01g
Total Fat	0.21g	Carbohydrates	0.42g
Saturated Fat	0g	Cholesterol	0mg
Sodium	28.42mg	Fiber	0g

FRUITED CHEESE SPREAD

1. 1 Package (8 oz.) Fat Free Cream Cheese
    (room temperature)
2. 1 Tablespoon Concentrated Orange Juice (defrosted)
3. Few Drops Vanilla Extract

Combine above ingredients and mix well. Spread on toast
rounds or slices of high fiber bread cut in fourths.

PER TABLESPOON:

Calories	15.86	Protein	1.74g
Total Fat	0g	Carbohydrates	2.03g
Saturated Fat	0g	Cholesterol	0mg
Sodium	63.56mg	Fiber	0.02g

PIMIENTO CREAM SPREAD

1. 2 Cups Lowfat Cottage Cheese
2. 1 Teaspoon Onion Powder
3. 1 Jar (3 oz.) Pimientos (drained)

Mix above ingredients in blender. Serve as a spread or
stuff celery stalks.

PER TABLESPOON:

Calories	9.35	Protein	1.49g
Total Fat	0.13g	Carbohydrates	0.51g
Saturated Fat	0.08g	Cholesterol	0.52mg
Sodium	47.95mg	Fiber	0.03g

PIMENTO CHEESE SPREAD

1. 1 Pound Fat Free Cheese (cubed)
2. 1 Jar (3 oz.) Pimentos (drained)
3. 1/2 Cup Fat Free Mayonnaise

Blend above ingredients until smooth. Spread on crackers or vegetables.

PER TABLESPOON:

Calories	16.24	Protein	3.14g
Total Fat	0g	Carbohydrates	0.88g
Saturated Fat	0g	Cholesterol	0mg
Sodium	29.30mg	Fiber	0g

TROPICAL CHEESE SPREAD

1. 1/2 Cup Fat Free Cottage Cheese
2. 1/4 Cup Crushed Pineapple (drained)
3. 1 Teaspoon Lemon Juice

Combine first three ingredients and mix in blender until smooth. Serve on cocktail rye bread or crackers.

PER TABLESPOON:

Calories	11.01	Protein	1.63g
Total Fat	0.04g	Carbohydrates	0.92g
Saturated Fat	0.03g	Cholesterol	0.63mg
Sodium	1.63mg	Fiber	0.04g

BAGEL CHIPS

1. 1 Lowfat Bagel (try assorted flavors)
2. No Fat Butter Spray
3. 1/8 Teaspoon Garlic Powder
4. 1/8 Teaspoon Cajun Seasoning

Slice bagel into 1/4-inch thick rounds. Place in microwave bowl and cook on high for one minute. Gently stir. Continue to microwave in one minute increments, stirring after each minute, approximately 3 minutes. Watch carefully. Chips should be crisp. (If over-microwaved char spots will appear.) Remove from microwave and spray with butter spray and sprinkle with garlic powder and cajun seasoning. Makes great chips for dips and spreads. 2 Servings.

PER SERVING:

Calories	135.0	Protein	4.00g
Total Fat	0.25g	Carbohydrates	29.00g
Saturated Fat	0g	Cholesterol	0mg
Sodium	283.4mg	Fiber	1.50g

POTATO SKINS

1. 4 Potatoes (baked)
2. 8 Ounces Reduced Fat Cheddar Cheese (grated)
3. 1 Cup Fat Free Sour Cream
4. 2 Tablespoons Chopped Green Onion

Cut each potato into quarters lengthwise. Scoop out pulp.
Spray potato skins with cooking spray and place on baking
pan. Bake at 425 degrees for 10 minutes. Turn and bake
for an additional 5-8 minutes or until crisp and light brown.
Remove from oven and place cheese, sour cream and
onions on each quarter. Return to oven and bake until
cheese melts.

PER QUARTER:

Calories	105.3	Protein	6.78g
Total Fat	2.53g	Carbohydrates	14.42g
Saturated Fat	0g	Cholesterol	10.00mg
Sodium	83.80mg	Fiber	1.18g

SHERRIED MEATBALLS

1. 2 Pounds Lean Ground Beef
2. 1 Cup Catsup
3. 1 Cup Cooking Sherry
4. 2 Tablespoons Brown Sugar

Heat oven to 350 degrees. Season ground beef to taste and shape into 1-inch meatballs. Place meatballs in oven for 30 minutes to brown. Remove meatballs from browning pan and place into a casserole. Mix remaining three ingredients and pour over meatballs. Bake an additional 30 minutes. Serve meatballs with sauce. 50 Meatballs.

PER MEATBALL:

Calories	61.42	Protein	4.57g
Total Fat	3.37g	Carbohydrates	1.85g
Saturated Fat	1.32g	Cholesterol	15.79mg
Sodium	71.45mg	Fiber	0.06g

MEXICAN MEATBALLS

1. 1 Pound Lean Ground Beef
2. 1 Package Taco Seasoning Mix
3. Salsa

Mix lean ground beef and taco seasoning and shape into 1-inch meatballs. Brown in skillet and place on paper towel to drain. Reheat in oven and serve with chilled salsa. 25 Meatballs.

PER MEATBALL:

Calories	57.17	Protein	4.58g
Total Fat	3.33g	Carbohydrates	1.90g
Saturated Fat	1.31g	Cholesterol	14.15mg
Sodium	129.4mg	Fiber	0g

PARTY DRUMMETTES

1. 2 Pounds Chicken Drummettes (skin removed)
2. 1/4 Cup Low Sodium Soy Sauce
3. 1/4 Cup Wine Vinegar
4. 1/4 Teaspoon Garlic Powder

Broil drummettes, 8 minutes one side, turn and broil 6 minutes on other side until browned. Combine drummettes with remaining ingredients in a shallow baking dish. Cover and bake at 350 degrees for 30 minutes or until tender. Makes 20 drummettes.

PER DRUMMETTE:

Calories	80.46	Protein	13.02g
Total Fat	2.57g	Carbohydrate	0.51g
Saturated Fat	0.67g	Cholesterol	42.18mg
Sodium	248.9mg	Fiber	0g

PIZZA STICKS

1. 1 Can Refrigerated Pillsbury Pizza Crust
2. I Can't Believe It's Not Butter Spray
3. 1/2 Teaspoon Garlic Powder
4. 1/2 Teaspoon Parsley Flakes

Unroll pizza dough and place in shallow baking pan. Spray both sides with butter spray. Sprinkle with garlic and parsley. Cut into 8 long strips. Bake at 425 degrees for 10-15 minutes. Turn strips over and bake additional 5-7 minutes. 4 Servings.

PER SERVING:

Calories	180.6	Protein	6.03g
Total Fat	2.50g	Carbohydrates	33.13g
Saturated Fat	0.50g	Cholesterol	0mg
Sodium	390.1mg	Fiber	1.00g

MINI HEROES

1. 1 Container Pillsbury Dinner Rolls
2. 2 Tablespoons Dijon Mustard
3. 1 Package (6 oz.) Healthy Choice Smoked Ham
4. 1/2 Cup Healthy Choice NonFat Pizza Cheese

Place rolls on sprayed baking sheet. Stretch rolls to form a 4-inch circle. Combine mustard, ham and cheese. Place mixture in center of roll, dividing equally. Fold roll over in center and seal by pressing edge with a fork. Bake at 375 degrees for 15-18 minutes. 8 Servings.

PER SERVING:

Calories	147.5	Protein	10.63g
Total Fat	2.56g	Carbohydrates	18.88g
Saturated Fat	0.19g	Cholesterol	10.63mg
Sodium	586.3mg	Fiber	1.00g

GREEN CHILI PIE

1. 1 Can (4.5 oz.) Green Chilies (diced)
2. 2 Cups Healthy Choice NonFat Pizza Cheese
3. 1 Container (4 oz.) Egg Beaters (equal 2 eggs)
4. 2 Green Onions (chopped)

Place green chilies in a 7 1/2x11 1/2-inch oven proof casserole. Sprinkle with cheese and onions. Pour eggs over top. Sprinkle with paprika for garnish. Bake at 350 degrees for 10-15 minutes. 15 Servings.

PER SERVING:

Calories	30.36	Protein	5.78g
Total Fat	0g	Carbohydrates	1.52g
Saturated Fat	0g	Cholesterol	2.68mg
Sodium	155.2mg	Fiber	0.32g

SALMON PINWHEELS

1. 6 Fat Free Flour Tortillas
2. 1 Container (6 oz.) Salmon Flavored Fat Free Cream Cheese
3. 1/2 Cup Salmon (flaked, bones and skin removed)
4. 2 Green Onions (chopped)

Combine cream cheese, salmon and onions. Spread each tortilla with mixture and roll. Place in airtight container and refrigerate. Before serving, remove and slice across tortilla every inch. Makes 36 pinwheels - 2 per serving.

PER SERVING:

Calories	46.70	Protein	3.95g
Total Fat	0.56g	Carbohydrates	6.38g
Saturated Fat	0.11g	Cholesterol	6.07mg
Sodium	180.5mg	Fiber	0.02g

SALADS

APPLE COLESLAW

1. 2 Cups Cabbage (shredded)
2. 2 Medium Apples (cored, diced)
3. 1 Can (16 oz.) Crushed Pineapple (drained)
4. 3/4 Cup Fat Free Mayonnaise

Combine above ingredients, cover and refrigerate 1 hour or more before serving. 8 Servings.

PER SERVING:

Calories	60.87	Protein	0.56g
Total Fat	0.22g	Carbohydrate	15.42g
Saturated Fat	0.03g	Cholesterol	0mg
Sodium	288.7mg	Fiber	1.7g

APPLE SALAD WITH FETA CHEESE

1. 1 Large Head Bibb Lettuce (torn in bite-sized pieces)
2. 1 Large Red Delicious Apple (diced)
3. 2 Ounces Feta Cheese (crumbled)
4. 1/4 Cup Pritikin Fat Free Rasberry Vinaigrette

Dice apples right before before serving and toss with Rasberry Vinaigrette. Combine with other ingredients. 4 Servings.

PER SERVING:

Calories	82.01	Protein	2.21g
Total Fat	3.17g	Carbohydrate	11.69g
Saturated Fat	2.14g	Cholesterol	12.62mg
Sodium	194.1mg	Fiber	1.12g

BEET AND ONION SALAD

1. 1/4 Cup Wine Vinegar
2. 1 Teaspoon Sugar
3. 1 Can (16 oz.) Sliced Beets (undrained)
4. 1/2 Onion (sliced in rings)

Combine above ingredients and marinate at room temperature at least 30 minutes before serving. Stir every 10 minutes. 8 Servings.

PER SERVING:

Calories	24.36	Protein	0.63g
Total Fat	0.10g	Carbohydrate	5.89g
Saturated Fat	0.02g	Cholesterol	0mg
Sodium	155.7mg	Fiber	1.20g

BROCCOLI SALAD

1. 1 Bunch Fresh Broccoli Spears
2. 2 Ounces Feta Cheese
3. 1/2 Head Lettuce (torn in bite-sized pieces)
4. 1/2 Cup Fat Free Salad Dressing

Combine above ingredients and serve. 6 Servings.

PER SERVING:

Calories	60.90	Protein	3.72g
Total Fat	2.29g	Carbohydrate	7.26g
Saturated Fat	1.45g	Cholesterol	8.38mg
Sodium	292.6mg	Fiber	0.19g

CARROT RAISIN CELERY SALAD

1. 6 Cups Carrots (grated)
2. 1 Cup Raisins
3. 2 Cups Celery (sliced)
4. 1/3 Cup Fat Free Mayonnaise

Mix above ingredients and chill at least 1 hour. 8 Servings.

PER SERVING:

Calories	101.3	Protein	1.66g
Total Fat	0.28g	Carbohydrate	25.12g
Saturated Fat	0.06g	Cholesterol	0mg
Sodium	139.7mg	Fiber	3.71g

MARINATED CAULIFLOWER SALAD

1. 1 Head Cauliflower (divided into flowers and thinly sliced)
2. 1 Small Onion (thinly sliced)
3. 12 Small Pimiento-stuffed Olives (sliced)
4. 1/3 Cup Kraft Fat Free Catalina Salad Dressing

Mix all ingredients, cover and refrigerate at least 1 hour before serving. Stir occasionally. 8 Servings.

PER SERVING:

Calories	33.11	Protein	1.11g
Total Fat	0.75g	Carbohydrate	5.69g
Saturated Fat	0.02g	Cholesterol	0mg
Sodium	164.5mg	Fiber	1.43g

CUCUMBER SALAD

1. 1/4 Cup White Vinegar
2. 1 Tablespoon Honey
3. 1/2 Medium Green Pepper (diced)
4. 4 Medium Cucumbers (peeled, thinly sliced)

Combine vinegar and honey and pour over cucumbers and green peppers. Chill for several hours before serving. 8 Servings.

PER SERVING:

Calories	17.48	Protein	0.42g
Total Fat	0.08g	Carbohydrate	4.44g
Saturated Fat	0.02g	Cholesterol	0mg
Sodium	1.35mg	Fiber	0.53g

CUCUMBER STRAWBERRY SALAD

1. 1/4 Cup Fresh Lime Juice
2. 1 Small Green Pepper (diced)
3. 1 Cucumber (peeled, sliced)
4. 2 Cups Fresh or Frozen Strawberries (quartered)

Combine lime juice and pepper. Toss mixture with cucumbers and strawberries. Chill before serving. 4 Servings.

PER SERVING:

Calories	34.88	Protein	0.87g
Total Fat	0.36g	Carbohydrate	8.52g
Saturated Fat	0.03g	Cholesterol	0mg
Sodium	1.79mg	Fiber	2.32g

SWEET AND SOUR CUCUMBER SALAD

1. 2 Medium Cucumbers (peeled, sliced)
2. 1 Teaspoon Salt
3. 1 Tablespoon Vinegar
4. 3 Tablespoons Sugar

Place sliced cucumbers in bowl and mix well with salt. Let stand 15 minutes. Drain off all the salty fluid. Add vinegar and sugar and let stand 10 minutes. Before serving, drain sweet and sour juice from cucumber slices and place cucumbers into a serving bowl. 4 Servings.

PER SERVING:

Calories	42.11	Protein	0.36g
Total Fat	0.07g	Carbohydrate	10.65g
Saturated Fat	0.02g	Cholesterol	0mg
Sodium	582.5mg	Fiber	0.42g

FRUIT SALAD

1. 1 Can (20 oz.) Pineapple Chunks (drained)
2. 2 Cans (11 oz.) Mandarin Oranges (drained)
3. 1 Cup Miniature Marshmallows
4. 1/3 Cup Fat Free Mayonnaise

Toss together above ingredients and refrigerate. 6 Servings.

PER SERVING:

Calories	125.6	Protein	0.80g
Total Fat	0.02g	Carbohydrate	31.11g
Saturated Fat	0g	Cholesterol	0mg
Sodium	133.6mg	Fiber	1.33g

MEDLEY OF FRUIT

1. 1 Jar (26 oz.) Mango Wedges (drained, chopped)
2. 2 Medium Kiwi Fruits (pared, thinly sliced)
3. 2 Medium Bananas (thinly sliced)
4. 1 Teaspoon Lemon Juice

Toss above ingredients in lemon juice and chill.
8 Servings.

PER SERVING:

Calories	119.2	Protein	0.48g
Total Fat	0.63g	Carbohydrate	29.87g
Saturated Fat	0.05g	Cholesterol	0mg
Sodium	5.30mg	Fiber	1.33g

GREEN BEAN AND BABY CORN SALAD

1. 1 Pound Green Beans (trimmed)
2. 1 Can (7 oz.) Pickled Baby Ears of Corn (undrained)
3. 4 Green Onion (sliced)

Blanch beans for 5-6 minutes in salted water until crisp tender. Drain, rinse and cool. Combine with baby corn and onions. Juice from corn acts as dressing. Toss and chill. 6 Servings.

PER SERVING:

Calories	36.35	Protein	2.68g
Total Fat	0.11g	Carbohydrate	7.12g
Saturated Fat	0.02g	Cholesterol	0mg
Sodium	110.4mg	Fiber	3.93g

HEARTS OF PALM SALAD

1. 2 Heads Boston Lettuce (torn in bite-sized pieces)
2. 6 Green Onions (sliced)
3. 1 Can (14 oz.) Hearts of Palm
   (drained, sliced horizontally)
4. 1/2 Cup Lowfat Viniagrette Dressing

Toss lettuce, onions and hearts of palm. Pour over salad and serve with viniagrette dressing. 6 Servings.

PER SERVING:

Calories	36.27	Protein	1.41
Total Fat	1.93g	Carbohydrate	3.73g
Saturated Fat	0.26g	Cholesterol	1.15mg
Sodium	387.7mg	Fiber	1.56g

SNOW PEA SALAD

1. 2 Cups Snow Peas (trimmed)
2. 1 Red Bell Pepper (sliced)
3. 1 Teaspoon Toasted Sesame Seeds
4. 1/2 Cup Hidden Valley Fat Free Italian Parmesan
   Salad Dressing

Blanch the snow peas and drain, running under cold water. Pat dry and refrigerate for an hour. When ready to serve, place snows peas in a circle on individual plates.
Arrange red pepper strips between snow peas and sprinkle with sesame seeds. Drizzle salad dressing over top of each salad. 4 Servings.

PER SERVING:

Calories	63.68	Protein	2.44g
Total Fat	0.76g	Carbohydrate	11.36g
Saturated Fat	0.11g	Cholesterol	0mg
Sodium	243.5mg	Fiber	2.54g

BELL PEPPER SALAD

1. 1 Medium Red Bell Pepper (sliced)
2. 1 Medium Green Bell Pepper (sliced)
3. 1 Medium Yellow Bell Pepper (sliced)
4. 1/4 Cup Fat Free Vinaigrette Dressing

Mix peppers in large bowl and toss with dressing. Refrigerate until ready to serve. 6 Servings.

PER SERVING:

Calories	30.42	Protein	1.06g
Total Fat	0.22g	Carbohydrate	7.16g
Saturated Fat	0.01g	Cholesterol	0mg
Sodium	10.23mg	Fiber	0.94g

HEARTY SPINACH AND MUSHROOM SALAD

1. 1 Bag (10 oz.) Cold Water Washed Spinach (torn in bite-sized pieces)
2. 1 Package (8 oz.) Sliced Mushrooms
3. 1 Medium Zucchini (sliced)
4. 1/2 Cup Fat Free Red Wine Vinegar Dressing

In large bowl, toss spinach, mushrooms and zucchini. Add dressing and toss again. 8 Servings.

PER SERVING:

Calories	39.66	Protein	1.79g
Total Fat	0.27g	Carbohydrate	8.53g
Saturated Fat	0.04g	Cholesterol	0mg
Sodium	64.62mg	Fiber	1.49g

SUNSHINE SALAD

1. 1 Package (10 oz.) Cold Water Washed Spinach
   (torn bite-sized pieces)
2. 2 Navel Oranges (peeled, sectioned, cut in half)
3. 1/2 Red Onion (thinly sliced)
4. 1/2 Cup Fat Free Fruited Salad Dressing
   (Paul's No Oil Tangerine and Mint Dressing)

Mix spinach, oranges, and red onion. Toss with dressing
and chill until ready to serve. 8 Servings.

PER SERVING:

Calories	31.99	Protein	1.44g
Total Fat	0.18g	Carbohydrate	6.95g
Saturated Fat	0.03g	Cholesterol	0mg
Sodium	40.30mg	Fiber	1.92g

TANGY SPINACH SALAD

1. 1 Package (10 oz.) Cold Water Washed Spinach
   (torn in bite-sized pieces)
2. 1 Cup Lowfat Cottage Cheese
3. 1 Red Bell Pepper (thinly sliced)
4. 1/2 Cup Fat Free Honey Mustard Salad Dressing

Combine above ingredients and toss with dressing. 8 Servings.

PER SERVING:

Calories	55.74	Protein	5.18g
Total Fat	0.45g	Carbohydrate	8.20g
Saturated Fat	0.21g	Cholesterol	1.24mg
Sodium	238.1mg	Fiber	1.33g

SPINACH WITH SPROUTS

1. 1 Package (10 oz.) Cold Water Washed Spinach (torn bite-size pieces)
2. 2 Cups Fresh Bean Sprouts
3. 1 Can (8 1/2 oz.) Water Chestnuts (sliced, drained)
4. 1/2 Cup Fat·Free Mayonnaise

Mix above ingredients and serve. 8 Servings.

PER SERVING:

Calories	40.66	Protein	2.07g
Total Fat	0.19g	Carbohydrate	8.53g
Saturated Fat	0.03g	Cholesterol	0mg
Sodium	157.1mg	Fiber	1.42g

FRUIT AND SPINACH SALAD

1. 1 Package (10 oz.) Cold Water Washed Spinach (torn in bite-sized pieces)
2. 1 Large Red Delicious Apple (cored, chopped)
3. 1 Medium Pear (cored, chopped)
4. 4 Green Onions (sliced)

Combine above ingredients and toss with a fruited fat free viniagrette dressing. 8 Servings.

PER SERVING:

Calories	54.64	Protein	1.24g
Total Fat	0.28g	Carbohydrate	12.95g
Saturated Fat	0.04g	Cholesterol	0mg
Sodium	63.96mg	Fiber	2.08g

SPINACH CHICKEN SALAD

1. 2 Packages (10 oz.) Frozen Chopped Spinach
2. 1 Pound Chicken Breasts (cooked, skinless, boneless)
3. 2 Tablespoons Lemon Pepper
4. 1 Cup Fat Free Mayonnaise

Thaw spinach and pat dry with paper towel. Place in large bowl. Shred chicken breasts and add to spinach. Toss spinach and chicken with lemon pepper and mayonnaise. 6 Servings.

PER SERVING:

Calories	172.5	Protein	26.21g
Total Fat	3.04g	Carbohydrate	8.66g
Saturated Fat	0.82g	Cholesterol	64.39mg
Sodium	464.9mg	Fiber	2.56g

SWEET POTATO SALAD

1. 3 Sweet Potatoes (approximately 1/2 lb. each)
2. 1 Medium Onion (sliced into thin rings)
3. 1 Green Pepper (cut into thin strips)
4. 1/4 Cup Fat Free Vinaigrette Dressing

Heat enough water to boiling to cover sweet potatoes. Add sweet potatoes and return to boil. Cover and cook 30 minutes or just until fork tender. Do not overcook. Cool and slice into 1/4-inch slices. Combine sweet potato slices, onion rings and green pepper strips in large bowl. Refrigerate at least one hour. Toss lightly with vinaigrette dressing. 8 Servings.

PER SERVING:

Calories	105.5	Protein	1.80g
Total Fat	0.32g	Carbohydrate	24.29g
Saturated Fat	0.06g	Cholesterol	0mg
Sodium	108.0mg	Fiber	2.82g

ROMAINE STRAWBERRY SALAD

1. 1 Head Romaine Lettuce (torn into bite-size pieces)
2. 1 Cup Fresh Strawberries (sliced)
3. 1/2 Purple Onion (coarsely chopped)
4. 1/4 Cup Pritikin Raspberry Vinaigrette Dressing

Combine first three ingredients and toss gently. Serve with raspberry vinaigrette salad dressing. 6 Servings.

PER SERVING:

Calories	29.17	Protein	0.47g
Total Fat	0.13g	Carbohydrate	6.81g
Saturated Fat	0.01g	Cholesterol	0mg
Sodium	24.83mg	Fiber	1.05g

ITALIAN TOMATO CHEESE SALAD

1. 12 Cherry Tomatoes (cut in halves)
2. 1 Ounce Mozzarella Cheese (cut in cubes)
3. 4 Pitted Black Olives (sliced)
4. 1 Tablespoon Fat Free Italian Salad Dressing

Mix above ingredients and toss lightly to coat with dressing. Refrigerate until chilled. Serve on a bed of lettuce. 4 Servings.

PER SERVING:

Calories	52.21	Protein	2.82g
Total Fat	2.59g	Carbohydrate	5.38g
Saturated Fat	0.95g	Cholesterol	3.83mg
Sodium	185.4	Fiber	1.01g

TURKEY SALAD

1. 3 Cups Cooked Cubed Turkey Breasts
2. 1 Can (16 oz.) Pineapple Tidbits (drained)
3. 1 Can (8 oz.) Sliced Water Chestnuts (drained)
4. 4 Green Onions (sliced)

Combine above ingredients and serve with a fat free honey mustard dressing. 6 Servings.

PER SERVING:

Calories	161.8	Protein	22.53g
Total Fat	0.04g	Carbohydrate	17.32g
Saturated Fat	0g	Cholesterol	501.0mg
Sodium	946.4mg	Fiber	0.88g

LUNCHEON TUNA SALAD

1. 1 Can (10 oz.) Water-Packed Tuna (drained)
2. 1 Can (8 oz.) Peas (drained)
3. 3/4 Cup Celery (finely chopped)
4. 1/2 Cup Fat Free Mayonnaise

Toss all ingredients and chill. Serve on a bed of lettuce. 4 Servings.

PER SERVING:

Calories	159.1	Protein	21.57g
Total Fat	1.97g	Carbohydrate	11.95g
Saturated Fat	0.51g	Cholesterol	29.77mg
Sodium	671.6mg	Fiber	2.71g

MARINATED VEGETABLE SALAD

1. 2 Cups Cauliflower Pieces
2. 2 Cups Broccoli Pieces
3. 1 Basket Cherry Tomatoes (cut in halves)
4. 1 Bottle (8 oz.) Fat Free Italian Dressing

Mix above ingredients and chill overnight. 6 Servings.

PER SERVING:

Calories	43.64	Protein	2.02g
Total Fat	0.36g	Carbohydrate	8.43g
Saturated Fat	0.05g	Cholesterol	0mg
Sodium	553.3mg	Fiber	1.46g

Most fresh and frozen fruits and vegetables are naturally low in fat and calories and high in vitamins and minerals. Combine them with dressings and condiments that are low in fat or fat free and you can eat all you want.

VEGETABLES

TARRAGON ASPARAGUS

1. 1 Pound Fresh Asparagus Spears
2. I Can't Believe It's Not Butter Spray
3. 1 Tablespoon Tarragon
4. 1/4 Teaspoon Pepper

Wash asparagus and break off at tender point. Steam over boiling water for 6 minutes or until barely tender. Remove from heat and drain. Spray with butter spray and sprinkle with tarragon and pepper. 4 Servings.

PER SERVING:

Calories	26.08	Protein	2.59g
Total Fat	0.23g	Carbohydrate	5.15g
Saturated Fat	0.05g	Cholesterol	0mg
Sodium	2.27mg	Fiber	2.38g

ASPARAGUS WITH SESAME SEEDS

1. 1 Pound Fresh Asparagus Spears
2. 2 Tablespoons Lime Juice
3. 1 Tablespoon Sesame Seeds
4. Garnish With Pimiento Strips

Wash asparagus and break off at tender point. In large saucepan bring 1/2 cup water to a boil and add asparagus. Cover and steam until just tender, around 6 minutes. Remove from heat and drain. Place on platter, decorate with pimiento strips and sprinkle with lime juice and sesame seeds. Serve warm or cold. 4 Servings.

PER SERVING:

Calories	41.83	Protein	3.21g
Total Fat	1.33g	Carbohydrate	6.44g
Saturated Fat	0.21g	Cholesterol	0mg
Sodium	3.14mg	Fiber	2.41g

DIJON BROCCOLI

1. 1 Cup Uncooked Pasta (about 4 ounces)
2. 1 Package (10 oz.) Frozen Chopped Broccoli
    (cooked and drained)
3. 1/4 Cup Lowfat Sour Cream
4. 2 Tablespoons Dijon Mustard

Cook pasta according to package directions. Drain.
Combine broccoli, sour cream and mustard with pasta.
Toss all ingredients until well mixed. Chill until ready to
serve. 4 Servings.

PER SERVING:

Calories	125.5	Protein	5.88g
Total Fat	1.68g	Carbohydrate	20.25g
Saturated Fat	0.11g	Cholesterol	25.42mg
Sodium	213.8mg	Fiber	2.13g

PARMESAN BROCCOLI AND MUSHROOMS

1. 1 Package (10 oz.) Frozen Chopped Broccoli
    (cooked and drained)
2. 1 Jar (4 1/2 oz.) Sliced Mushrooms (drained)
3. 2 Tablespoons Fat Free Margarine
4. 1/4 Cup Grated Parmesan Cheese

While broccoli is still warm, combine above ingredients.
Toss and serve. 4 Servings.

PER SERVING:

Calories	51.37	Protein	4.67
Total Fat	1.80g	Carbohydrate	5.16g
Saturated Fat	1.00g	Cholesteral	3.93mg
Sodium	290.6mg	Fiber	2.89g

LEMON BRUSSELS SPROUTS

1. 1 Package (10 oz.) Frozen Brussels Sprouts
2. 1/4 Cup Fat Free Margarine
3. 2 Teaspoons Chopped Parsley
4. 2 Teaspoons Grated Lemon Rind

Prepare brussel sprouts according to package directions. Drain and place in serving bowl. In small saucepan, melt margarine and stir in parsley and lemon rind. Heat and pour over sprouts. 4 Servings.

PER SERVING:

Calories	34.95	Protein	2.70g
Total Fat	0.29g	Carbohydrate	5.61g
Saturated Fat	0.06g	Cholesterol	0.06mg
Sodium	97.35mg	Fiber	2.69g

MINTED CARROTS

1. 3 Cups Sliced Carrots
2. 1 Tablespoon Honey
3. 1 Teaspoon Fresh or Dried Mint Leaves
4. Butter Spray

Heat 1-inch water to boiling and add carrots. When water returns to boiling, reduce heat and cover. Cook carrots until crisp-tender, around 10 minutes. Drain and toss with honey, mint and butter spray. 4 Servings.

PER SERVING:

Calories	53.40	Protein	1.06g
Total Fat	0.20g	Carbohydrate	12.96g
Saturated Fat	0.04g	Cholesterol	0mg
Sodium	56.85mg	Fiber	3.08g

HONEY CARROTS

1. 4 Cups Baby Carrots
2. 2 Tablespoon Brown Sugar (firmly packed)
3. 2 Tablespoons Honey
4. 2 Tablespoons Fat Free Margarine

Combine brown sugar, margarine and honey in saucepan and stir until melted. Place carrots in oven proof casserole with cover. Pour honey mixture over carrots and toss. Bake at 400 degrees for one hour. Stir occassionally to coat carrots with honey mixture. 8 Servings.

PER SERVING:

Calories	54.09	Protein	0.64g
Total Fat	0.40g	Carbohydrate	12.62g
Saturated Fat	0.07g	Cholesterol	0mg
Sodium	49.71mg	Fiber	22.40g

GINGER CARROTS

1. 1 Pound Package Mini Carrots
2. 1 Teaspoon Brown Sugar
3. 1 Teaspoon Fat Free Margarine
4. 1/8 Teaspoon Ground Ginger

Place carrots in steam rack over boiling water and steam around 10 minutes. Remove from heat and set aside. In saucepan, melt margarine and add brown sugar and ginger. Cook over low heat, stirring constantly, until sugar is dissolved. Add carrots and stir gently until carrots are well coated and heated thoroughly. 4 Servings.

PER SERVING:

Calories	46.35	Protein	0.95g
Total Fat	0.60g	Carbohydrate	9.99g
Saturated Fat	0.10g	Cholesterol	0mg
Sodium	47.48mg	Fiber	0g

CARROTS AND ZUCCHINI

1. 3 Medium Carrots (peeled and sliced)
2. 1 Medium Zucchini (sliced)
3. 1/2 Cup Chicken Broth
4. 1 Teaspoon Italian Seasoning

In saucepan cook carrots and zucchini in chicken broth until just tender. Drain and return vegetables to saucepan. Add seasoning and toss gently. 4 Servings.

PER SERVING:

Calories	24.89	Protein	1.23g
Total Fat	0.27g	Carbohydrate	4.77g
Saturated Fat	0.07g	Cholesterol	0mg
Sodium	111.9mg	Fiber	1.43g

CARROT CASSEROLE

1. 1 Package (1 lb.) Mini Carrots (sliced)
2. 1/2 Cup Lowfat Swiss Cheese (shredded)
3. 1/4 Teaspoon Ground Nutmeg
4. 1 Cup Fat Free Chicken Broth

Cook carrots in broth until tender. Drain and retain broth. Mash carrots. Combine mashed carrots, cheese and nutmeg. Add some of the broth (1/2 cup) to make carrots creamy. Place in casserole and bake at 350 degrees for 15-20 minutes. 4 Servings.

PER SERVING:

Calories	96.26	Protein	6.17g
Total Fat	2.72g	Carbohydrate	11.75g
Saturated Fat	0.03g	Cholesterol	8.50mg
Sodium	254.7mg	Fiber	3.40g

BRAISED CELERY

1. 2 Cups Celery Sticks
2. 1/2 Cup Beef Bouillon
3. 2 Tablespoons Chopped Fresh Parsley
4. 1 Tablespoon Lowfat Margarine

Combine above ingredients and place in 1 quart casserole.
Bake at 400 degrees for 30 minutes. 4 Servings.

PER SERVING:

Calories	25.08	Protein	0.67g
Total Fat	1.56g	Carbohydrate	2.51g
Saturated Fat	0.29g	Cholesterol	0mg
Sodium	255.7mg	Fiber	1.02g

SOUTHWESTERN CORN

1. 2 Cans (15.25 oz.) Corn (drained)
2. 1 Red Bell Pepper (chopped)
3. 1/4 Cup Onions (chopped)
4. I Can't Believe It's Not Butter Spray

Spray nonstick skillet with butter spray. Saute pepper
and onions in butter spray until soft. Add corn and cook
over low heat for 10 minutes. 6 Servings.

PER SERVING:

Calories	122.9	Protein	3.97g
Total Fat	1.48g	Carbohydrate	28.23g
Saturated Fat	0.23g	Cholesterol	0mg
Sodium	466.9mg	Fiber	3.26g

SPICY CORN BAKE

1. 2 Cans (15.25 oz.) Corn (drained)
2. 1/2 Cup Onion (sliced)
3. 1 Tablespoon Prepared Mustard
4. 1/2 Cup Chili Sauce

Combine above ingredients and place into a casserole. Bake at 350 degrees for 25 minutes 6 Servings.

PER SERVING:

Calories	144.9	Protein	4.57g
Total Fat	1.55g	Carbohydrate	33.07g
Saturated Fat	0.23g	Cholesterol	0mg
Sodium	760.4mg	Fiber	3.14g

ITALIAN EGGPLANT

1. 1 Small Eggplant
2. 1/4 Cup Egg Beaters
3. 1/2 Cup Italian Seasoned Breadcrumbs
4. 1 1/2 Cup Spaghetti Sauce

Spray nonstick skillet with cooking spray. Remove peel of eggplant and slice into circles. Dip circle in egg beater then into breadcrumbs. Place each round in skillet and brown on both sides. Place in ovenproof casserole, putting a generous tablespoon of spaghetti sauce on each eggplant round. Stack if necessary. Bake covered at 350 degrees for 30 minutes. 4 Servings.

PER SERVING:

Calories	121.4	Protein	5.06g
Total Fat	2.65g	Carbohydrate	19.34g
Saturated Fat	0.10g	Cholesterol	0.22mg
Sodium	872.8mg	Fiber	1.20g

GARLIC GREEN BEANS

1. 1 Package (10 oz.) Frozen Italian-style Green Beans
2. 2 Teaspoons Olive Oil
3. 2 Garlic Cloves (crushed)
4. 2 Tablespoons Grated Parmesan Cheese

In nonstick skillet over medium heat, combine beans, olive oil and garlic. Bring to a boil. Cover, reduce heat and simmer 5 minutes. Remove cover, stir and cook 3 minutes longer or until liquid evaporates. Season to taste and sprinkle with parmesan cheese. 4 Servings.

PER SERVING:

Calories	61.97	Protein	2.10g
Total Fat	4.13g	Carbohydrate	4.93g
Saturated Fat	0.93g	Cholesterol	1.97mg
Sodium	56.04mg	Fiber	1.17g

GREEN BEANS WITH DILL

1. 2 Cans (14 1/2 oz.) French Style Green Beans
2. 1/2 Cup Fresh Mushrooms (sliced)
3. 1 Teaspoon Fat Free Margarine
4. 1 1/2 Teaspoon Dried Dill Weed

Warm beans over medium to low heat. Add mushrooms and cook 1 minute longer. Drain and toss with margarine and dill. 6 Servings.

PER SERVING:

Calories	22.33	Protein	1.29g
Total Fat	0.16g	Carbohydrate	5.08g
Saturated Fat	0.03g	Cholesterol	0mg
Sodium	7.99mg	Fiber	1.17g

TANGY ITALIAN MUSHROOMS

1. 2 Cups Fresh Mushrooms (sliced)
2. 1/2 Cup Fat Free Italian Dressing
3. 1 Large Onion (chopped)
3. Butter Spray

Marinate mushrooms in dressing for at least 1 hour or overnight, stirring occassionally. In non-stick skillet saute onion in butter spray. Drain mushrooms and add to onions. Continue to cook over medium heat until mushrooms are tender, but not limp. 6 Servings.

PER SERVING:

Calories	24.01	Protein	0.80g
Total Fat	0.14g	Carbohydrate	4.73g
Saturated Fat	0.02g	Cholesterol	0mg
Sodium	282.3mg	Fiber	0.76g

SCALLOPED POTATOES

1. 3 Medium Potatoes (thinly sliced)
2. 1/3 Cup Grated Parmesan Cheese
3. 2/3 Cup Skim Milk
4. 1/2 Teaspoon Paprika

Layer potatoes and cheese in a 2 quart casserole sprayed with cooking spray. Pour milk over potatoes and sprinkle with paprika. Cover and vent. Cook in microwave for 12 minutes. Take out, remove cover and broil 2-3 minutes to brown. 4 Servings.

PER SERVING:

Calories	146.2	Protein	6.33g
Total Fat	2.17g	Carbohydrate	25.79g
Saturated Fat	1.34g	Cholesterol	5.93mg
Sodium	148.7mg	Fiber	2.11g

HERBED NEW POTATOES

1. 2 Cans (15 oz.) New Potatoes
2. 1 Tablespoon Minced Parsley
3. 1 Tablespoon Minced Chives
4. 1 Tablespoon Fat Free Margarine

Heat potatoes in medium saucepan. Drain and add remaining ingredients, toss until potatoes are coated. 4 Servings.

PER SERVING:

Calories	86.30	Protein	2.89g
Total Fat	0.32g	Carbohydrate	18.41g
Saturated Fat	0.08g	Cholesterol	0mg
Sodium	662.5mg	Fiber	3.40g

POTATOES O'BRIEN

1. 2 Cans (15 oz.) Sliced New Potatoes (drained)
2. 1/2 Onion (finely minced)
3. 1/2 Green Pepper (diced)
4. 2 Tablespoons Fat Free Margarine

Melt margarine in non-stick skillet. Add onions and green pepper and cook over medium heat until tender. Add drained potatoes and continue to saute for 5 minutes. Pepper to taste. Place in 9-inch sprayed pie plate and bake for 15 minutes at 350 degrees. 4 Servings.

PER SERVING:

Calories	97.65	Protein	3.21g
Total Fat	0.37g	Carbohydrate	20.73g
Saturated Fat	0.09g	Cholesterol	0mg
Sodium	685.8mg	Fiber	3.93g

ROASTED NEW POTATOES

1. 4 Medium Sized New Potatoes (quartered)
2. 2 Tablespoons Fat Free Margarine
3. 3 Small Onions (quartered)
4. 1/2 Teaspoon Marjoram

Melt margarine and add to a 2-quart casserole. Stir in marjoram. Add potatoes and onions and toss in melted mixture until coated. Cover dish and bake at 400 degrees for 1 to 1 1/2 hours. 4 Servings.

PER SERVING:

Calories	81.76	Protein	1.81g
Total Fat	0.13g	Carbohydrate	18.29g
Saturated Fat	0.03g	Cholesterol	0mg
Sodium	49.02mg	Fiber	1.94g

SPICY NEW POTATOES

1. 8 Small New Potatoes
2. 1 Teaspoon Concentrated Instant Liquid Crab & Shrimp Boil
3. 4 Cups Water

Pour crab boil into water and bring to a boil. Puncture potatoes and add to boiling water. Reduce heat and simmer until potato skins barely pop and potatoes are tender, around 20 minutes. 4 Servings.

PER SERVING:

Calories	67.86	Protein	1.46g
Total Fat	0.08g	Carbohydrate	15.70g
Saturated Fat	0.02g	Cholesterol	0mg
Sodium	3.12mg	Fiber	1.40g

MASHED POTATOES AND CARROTS

1. 4 Potatoes (peeled, cut into chunks)
2. 1 Large Carrot (peeled, cut into chunks)
3. 1/3 Cup Skim Milk
4. 1 Teaspoon Dried Dill Leaves

In boiling water, add potatoes and carrot and cook for 25 minutes or until tender. Drain. Return to pot and mash. Stir in milk and dill. Season to taste. 6 Servings.

PER SERVING:

Calories	66.59	Protein	1.72g
Total Fat	0.11g	Carbohydrate	15.05g
Saturated Fat	0.04g	Cholesterol	0.24mg
Sodium	18.81mg	Fiber	1.60g

COTTAGE CHEESE STUFFED BAKED POTATOES

1. 2 Baking Potatoes (baked)
2. 1 Cup Lowfat Cottage Cheese
3. 1 Tablespoon Chives
4. 1 Teaspoon Onion Powder

Bake potatoes in 425 degrees oven for 1 hour. Cut potatoes in half lengthwise and scoop out insides. Return shell to oven and bake until crisp. Whip potato insides with remaining ingredients and put mixture into potato skins. Return to oven and bake until thoroughly heated.
4 Servings.

PER SERVING:

Calories	151.0	Protein	9.32g
Total Fat	0.68g	Carbohydrate	27.02g
Saturated Fat	0.39g	Cholesterol	2.49mg
Sodium	237.5mg	Fiber	2.42g

STUFFED BAKED POTATOES

1. 4 Baking Potatoes (baked)
2. 1/2 Cup Skim Milk
3. 2 Tablespoons Fat Free Margarine
4. 1/4 Cup Lowfat Cheddar Cheese

Cut baked potatoes in half lengthwise. Scoop potato out of skin leaving shell intact. Mash potato pulp with milk and margarine. Stir in cheese. Refill potato shells with mixture and reheat briefly at 350 degrees until warm. 8 Servings.

PER SERVING:

Calories	136.7	Protein	4.85g
Total Fat	1.38g	Carbohydrate	26.47g
Saturated Fat	0.04g	Cholesterol	5.28mg
Sodium	73.47mg	Fiber	2.42g

GINGERED SWEET POTATOES

1. 2 Medium Sweet Potatoes (peeled, diced)
2. 1 Tablespoon Lowfat Margarine
3. 1 Teaspoon Brown Sugar
4. 1/4 Teaspoon Ground Ginger or Pumpkin Pie Spice

Arrange potatoes in a steaming rack. Place over boiling water; cover and steam until tender. Remove and place in serving dish. Combine remaining ingredients, blend well. Toss with the hot sweet potatoes. 4 Servings.

PER SERVING:

Calories	193.2	Protein	2.71g
Total Fat	1.87g	Carbohydrate	42.02g
Saturated Fat	0.33g	Cholesterol	0mg
Sodium	54.70mg	Fiber	4.10g

BAKED SWEET POTATOES

1. 2 Cans (15 oz.) Sweet Potatoes With Juice
   (cut into 1/2-inch chunks)
2. 1/2 Cup Brown Sugar (firmly packed)
3. 1/4 Cup Fat Free Margarine (melted)
4. 1/2 Teaspoon Cinnamon

Layer potatoes, brown sugar and margarine in a casserole. Sprinkle with cinnamon. Bake uncovered at 375 degrees for 30 minutes. 8 Servings.

PER SERVING:

Calories	131.6	Protein	1.05g
Total Fat	0.22g	Carbohydrate	31.18g
Saturated Fat	0.05g	Cholesterol	0mg
Sodium	95.35mg	Fiber	1.99g

COTTAGED SWEET POTATOES

1. 4 Sweet Potatoes (peeled, cut into strips)
2. 2 Tablespoons Vegetable Oil
3. 2 Tablespoons Cajun Spice Seasoning
4. 1 Tablespoon Hot Pepper Sauce

Mix oil, cajun spice and hot pepper sauce together. Add potatoes and toss until well coated. Spread potatoes onto a nonstick pan sprayed lightly with cooking spray. Bake at 400 degrees for 40 minutes, turning occasionally or until potatoes are tender. 8 Servings.

PER SERVING:

Calories	133.1	Protein	1.72g
Total Fat	3.52g	Carbohydrate	24.27g
Saturated Fat	0.42g	Cholesterol	0mg
Sodium	1015mg	Fiber	3.00g

GARLIC AND HERB CHEESE RICE

1. 1 Can (14 1/2 oz.) Fat Free Chicken Broth
2. 1 Cup Instant Rice
3. 1 Package (5 oz.) Light Garlic and Herb
   Soft Spreadable Cheese
4. 1/4 Teaspoon Ground Pepper

Bring chicken broth to a boil and gradually stir in rice.
Cook rice according to instructions on box. Remove from
heat and stir in cheese and pepper until cheese is melted.
4 Servings.

PER SERVING:

Calories	170.8	Protein	4.35g
Total Fat	5.07g	Carbohydrate	23.10g
Saturated Fat	3.15g	Cholesterol	12.50mg
Sodium	574.3mg	Fiber	0.42g

SESAME RICE

1. 4 Cups White Rice (cooked)
2. 1/4 Cup Green Onions (chopped)
3. 2 Tablespoon Sesame Seeds
4. 1/4 Cup Low Sodium Soy Sauce

While rice is still hot, combine all ingredients and place
into serving dish. Stir well. 8 Servings.

PER SERVING:

Calories	151.8	Protein	2.99g
Total Fat	1.30g	Carbohydrate	30.66g
Saturated Fat	0.21g	Cholesterol	0mg
Sodium	283.3mg	Fiber	0.08g

VEGGIE RICE

1. 3 Cups Brown Rice (cooked)
2. 1 Can (9 oz.) Peas (drained)
3. 2 Tablespoons Parsley
4. 2 Tablespoons Lowfat Margarine

In medium saucepan, combine ingredients. Stir until the mixture is heated through. 6 Servings.

PER SERVING:

Calories	115.5	Protein	4.46g
Total Fat	2.88g	Carbohydrate	29.96g
Saturated Fat	0.50g	Cholesterol	0mg
Sodium	142.2mg	Fiber	3.51g

SHERRIED BROWN RICE PILAF

1. 1 Cup Brown Rice (uncooked)
2. 2 Cups Fat Free Chicken Broth (plus 1 cup water)
3. 3/4 Cup Fresh Mushrooms (sliced)
4. 3 Tablespoons Cooking Sherry

In medium saucepan cook mushrooms in 2 tablespoons of water until slightly tender. Add rice. Stir in broth/water mixture and bring to a boil. Place into a 2-quart casserole, cover and bake at 350 degrees for 1 hour. Remove from heat and stir in sherry. Serve warm. 4 Servings.

PER SERVING:

Calories	191.9	Protein	3.95g
Total Fat	1.40g	Carbohydrate	37.08g
Saturated Fat	0.28g	Cholesterol	0mg
Sodium	374.7mg	Fiber	1.77g

SKILLET SQUASH

1. 1 Medium Acorn Squash
2. 1/3 Cup Pineapple Juice
3. 1 Tablespoon Light Brown Sugar
4. 1/4 Teaspoon Cinnamon

Cut squash crosswise into 1/2-inch slices and discard seeds. Arrange in large skillet. In small bowl, combine juice, sugar and cinnamon. Pour over squash rings. Bring to a boil and reduce heat. Simmer, covered, for 25 minutes or until squash is tender. Arrange squash on platter and pour remaining sauce over squash. 4 Servings.

PER SERVING:

Calories	80.31	Protein	1.21g
Total Fat	0.16g	Carbohydrate	20.83g
Saturated Fat	0.03g	Cholesterol	0mg
Sodium	4.32mg	Fiber	0.10g

CANDIED ACORN SQUASH

1. 2 Acorn Squash
2. 4 Tablespoons "lite" Maple Surup
3. 2 Teaspoons Lowfat Margarine
4. 1/4 Teaspoon Ground Allspice

Cut squash in half and remove seeds and stringy parts. Place halves, cut side up, in baking dish. Put 1 tablespoon syrup and 1/2 teaspoon margarine in each half. Sprinkle with allspice, cover and bake at 375 degrees for 35 minutes. 8 Servings.

PER SERVING:

Calories	74.79	Protein	1.17g
Total Fat	0.63g	Carbohydrate	18.15g
Saturated Fat	0.10g	Cholesterol	0mg
Sodium	37.91mg	Fiber	2.0g

SPINACH TOPPED TOMATOES

1. 1 Package (10 oz.) Chopped Spinach (cooked, drained)
2. 1 Teaspoon Instant Chicken Bouillon
3. 1/4 Teaspoon Nutmeg
4. 3 Medium Tomatoes

Place spinach in medium bowl. Mix bouillon with 1/2 cup hot water. Combine spinach with broth and nutmeg. Cut tomatoes into halves crosswise and arrange, cut side up, on baking sheet. Top each tomato half with 1/6 of the spinach mixture. Bake at 325 degrees for 30 minutes or until tomatoes are tender, but retain their shape.
6 Servings.

PER SERVING:

Calories	28.23	Protein	2.17g
Total Fat	0.35g	Carbohydrate	5.64g
Saturated Fat	0.06g	Cholesterol	0mg
Sodium	178.6mg	Fiber	2.10g

HERB TOMATO SLICES

1. 3 Medium Tomatoes
2. 2/3 Cups Fresh Bread Crumbs
3. 1 Tablespoon Fat Free Margarine (melted)
4. 1/4 Teaspoon Dried Basil

Slice tomatoes and place in shallow baking dish. Mix bread crumbs, margarine and basil. Sprinkle mixture over tomatoes and bake, uncovered, at 350 degrees for 5-6 minutes or until crumbs are brown. 6 Servings.

PER SERVING:

Calories	52.68	Protein	1.76g
Total Fat	0.74g	Carbohydrate	10.00g
Saturated Fat	0.15g	Cholesterol	0mg
Sodium	105.5mg	Fiber	1.09g

MARINATED VEGETABLES

1. 1 Package (10 oz.) Frozen Cut Green Beans
2. 1 Package (10 oz.) Frozen Cauliflower
3. 1/4 Cup Fat Free Italian Dressing
4. 1 Jar (2 oz.) Sliced Pimiento (drained)

Cook beans and cauliflower according to package directions. Drain vegetables and place in mixing bowl. Add salad dressing and pimiento. Toss until vegetables are coated. Cover and chill at least 4 hours or overnight. 8 Servings.

PER SERVING:

Calories	20.26	Protein	1.11g
Total Fat	0.10g	Carbohydrate	4.27g
Saturated Fat	0.01g	Cholesterol	0mg
Sodium	213.0mg	Fiber	1.35g

ZUCCHINI SQUASH

1. 2 Medium Zucchini Squash
2. I Can't Believe It's Not Butter Spray
3. 4 Teaspoons Parmesan Cheese
4. 4 Teaspoons Seasoned Bread Crumbs

Place zucchini on microwaveable dish. Pierce with fork. Microwave approximately 5 minutes on high or until tender but not soft. Split in half lengthwise. Spray with butter spray. Sprinkle each half with 1 teaspoon cheese and 1 teaspoon bread crumbs. 4 Servings.

PER SERVING:

Calories	23.43	Protein	1.71g
Total Fat	0.64g	Carbohydrates	3.24g
Saturated Fat	0.35g	Cholesterol	1.35mg
Sodium	81.56mg	Fiber	0.78g

Lowfat Recipe Samples From Volume I and II:

SQUASH CASSEROLE

1. 6 Medium Yellow Squash
2. 1 Small Onion (chopped)
3. 1 Cup Healthy Choice Fat Free Cheese
4. 1 Can (4 oz.) Chopped Green Chiles

Boil squash and onion until tender. Drain well and mix with cheese and chiles. Pour into dish sprayed with cooking spray. Bake 15 minutes at 375 degrees. 8 Servings.

PER SERVING:

Calories	44.55	Protein	5.44g
Total Fat	0.30g	Carbohydrates	5.74g
Saturated Fat	0.06g	Cholesterol	0mg
Sodium	56.20mg	Fiber	1.94g

OKRA SUCCOTASH (Volume II)

1. 3 Cups Okra (sliced)
2. 1 Can (16 oz.) Corn
3. 1 Can (14 1/2 oz.) Seasoned Stewed Tomatoes
4. 1/2 Cup Onion (chopped)

Rinse okra under running water. Drain. Combine ingredients in a large skillet. Cover and simmer for 15 minutes. Season to taste. 8 Servings.

PER SERVING:

Calories	67.26	Protein	2.38g
Total Fat	0.31g	Carbohydrates	15.47g
Saturated Fat	0.05g	Cholesterol	0mg
Sodium	293.0mg	Fiber	1.55g

CHICKEN

OVEN FRIED CHICKEN

1. 6 (5 oz.) Chicken Breasts (boneless, skinless)
2. 1 Cup Crushed Corn Flakes
3. 1/4 Cup Buttermilk
4. 1 Teaspoon Creole Seasoning

Combine creole seasoning and corn flake crumbs. Brush chicken with buttermilk and roll chicken in crumb mixture. Place chicken in baking dish and bake at 375 degrees for 1 hour. 6 Servings.

PER SERVING:

Calories	228.1	Protein	32.93g
Total Fat	2.65g	Carbohydrate	16.80g
Saturated Fat	2.56g	Cholesterol	40.44mg
Sodium	758.9mg	Fiber	0.49g

BROILED AND SPICY CHICKEN

1. 6 (5 oz.) Chicken Breasts (boneless, skinless)
2. 1/2 Cup Fat Free Italian Dressing
3. 1 Cup Tomato Juice
4. 1/2 Teaspoon Chili Powder

Combine dressing, tomato juice and chili powder. Pour over chicken and marinate for several hours. Broil for 30 minutes or until done, turning once and basting frequently. 6 Servings.

PER SERVING:

Calories	165.6	Protein	31.34g
Total Fat	2.56g	Carbohydrate	3.18g
Saturated Fat	2.50g	Cholesterol	40.00mg
Sodium	769.9mg	Fiber	0.24g

TARRAGON CHICKEN

1. 6 (5 oz.) Chicken Breasts (boneless, skinless)
2. 1 Cup White Cooking Wine
3. 1 Tablespoon Dried Tarragon Leaves
4. Black Pepper to Taste

Combine wine, tarragon and pepper. Pour over chicken and marinate for several hours in refrigerator. Bake chicken at 350 degrees for 1 hour. 6 Servings.

PER SERVING:

Calories	177.1	Protein	31.10g
Total Fat	2.51g	Carbohydrate	0.32g
Saturated Fat	2.51g	Cholesterol	40.08mg
Sodium	342.7mg	Fiber	0g

ORANGE MINT CHICKEN

1. 6 (5 oz.) Chicken Breasts (boneless, skinless)
2. 1 Cup Sugar Free Orange Marmalade
3. 2 Tablespoons Lemon Juice
4. 2 Teaspoon Dried Mint Leaves

In small saucepan, combine orange marmalade, lemon juice and mint leaves. Cook over low heat until glaze is well heated. Place chicken on shallow baking pan sprayed with cooking spray. Broil unglazed chicken breasts for 8 minutes on each side. Brush glaze over both sides of chicken and continue broiling for 15 minutes longer, turning once. Brush glaze over chicken breasts several times during last few minutes. 6 Servings.

PER SERVING:

Calories	215.3	Protein	31.02g
Total Fat	2.50g	Carbohydrate	15.80g
Saturated Fat	2.50g	Cholesterol	40.00mg
Sodium	340.1mg	Fiber	0.02g

LEMON GARLIC CHICKEN

1. 4 (5 oz.) Chicken Breasts (boneless, skinless)
2. 1 Clove Garlic (minced)
3. 1/2 Cup Fat Free Chicken Broth
4. 1 Tablespoon Lemon Juice

Using non-stick skillet sprayed with cooking spray, slowly saute garlic over low heat. Add chicken and cook over medium heat about 10 minutes or until brown on both sides. Add broth and lemon juice. Heat to boiling and then reduce heat. Cover and simmer 10-15 minutes or until chicken is done. Remove chicken and keep warm. Cook or reduce remaining liquid in pan, around 3 minutes. Pour over chicken and serve. 4 Servings.

PER SERVING:

Calories	153.3	Protein	31.06g
Total Fat	2.50g	Carbohydrate	0.70g
Saturated Fat	2.50g	Cholesterol	40.00mg
Sodium	432.7mg	Fiber	0.03g

CHICKEN BREASTS WITH MUSHROOMS

1. 6 (5 oz.) Chicken Breasts (boneless, skinless)
2 1 Tablespoon Basil
3. 1/4 Pound Fresh Mushrooms (sliced)
4. 3 Tablespoons White Cooking Wine

On stovetop place chicken breasts in non-stick skillet. Over low/medium heat brown chicken for 1-2 minutes. Add mushrooms, basil and wine and continue to cook for 30 minutes or until thoroughly cooked. Spoon sauce over breasts while cooking. 6 Servings.

PER SERVING:

Calories	159.9	Protein	31.41g
Total Fat	2.58g	Carbohydrate	0.96g
Saturated Fat	2.51g	Cholesterol	40.00mg
Sodium	341.1mg	Fiber	0.23g

CHERRY CHICKEN

1. 4 (5 oz.) Chicken Breasts (boneless, skinless)
2. 1 Tablespoon Lemon Juice
3. 1/3 Cup Cherry Preserves
4. Dash Ground Allspice

Pat chicken dry and place on rack of broiler pan. Broil 4-inches from heat for 6 minutes. Brush with lemon juice. Turn chicken over and brush with remaining juice and broil 6-9 minutes longer or until tender and no longer pink. In small saucepan heat cherry preserves and allspice. Spoon over chicken breasts and serve. 4 Servings.

PER SERVING:

Calories	214.8	Protein	31.20g
Total Fat	2.55g	Carbohydrate	17.33g
Saturated Fat	2.50g	Cholesterol	40.00mg
Sodium	350.6mg	Fiber	0.31g

SAVORY BAKED LEMON-CHICKEN

1. 6 (5 oz.) Chicken Breasts (boneless, skinless)
2. 1 Teaspoon Garlic Salt
3. Juice of 2 Lemons
4. 1/4 Cup Melted Fat Free Margarine

Rub chicken with garlic salt and lemon juice. Place in baking dish and pour margarine over chicken. Bake at 350 degrees for 1 hour, basting often. 6 Servings.

PER SERVING:

Calories	155.9	Protein	31.04g
Total Fat	2.50g	Carbohydate	0.88g
Saturated Fat	2.50g	Cholesterol	40.00mg
Sodium	560.5mg	Fiber	0.04g

LIME CHICKEN

1. 4 (5 oz.) Chicken Breasts (boneless, skinless)
2. Juice of Three Limes
3. 2 Tablespoons Garlic (chopped)
4. 2 Cups Mushrooms (sliced)

Slice chicken into thin strips. Saute chicken and garlic in lime juice until chicken is tender. Add mushrooms and continue to cook until chicken is lightly browned.
4 Servings.

PER SERVING:

Calories	175.5	Protein	32.28g
Total Fat	2.71g	Carbohydrate	6.05g
Saturated Fat	2.53g	Cholesterol	40.00mg
Sodium	342.8mg	Fiber	0.66g

HONEY CHICKEN

1. 6 (5 oz.) Chicken Breasts (boneless, skinless)
2. 1/2 Cup Honey
3. 1/3 Cup Lemon Juice
4. 1/4 Cup Soy Sauce

Combine honey, lemon juice and soy sauce. Brush chicken with half of the mixture and bake at 350 degrees for 20 minutes. Brush with additional mixture and bake for an additional 35 minutes or until done. Baste frequently. 6 Servings.

PER SERVING:

Calories	245.9	Protein	32.40g
Total Fat	2.51g	Carbohydrate	24.94g
Saturated Fat	2.50g	Cholesterol	40.00mg
Sodium	1013mg	Fiber	0.21g

OVEN BARBECUED CHICKEN

1. 4 (5 oz.) Chicken Breasts (boneless, skinless)
2. 1/2 Cup Jellied Cranberry Sauce
3. 1/4 Cup Tomato Sauce
4. 2 Tablespoon Prepared Mustard

Combine cranberry sauce, tomato sauce and mustard. Brush both sides of chicken breasts with mixture. Bake, uncovered, at 375 degrees for 30 minutes. Turn chicken, brush with barbecue mixture again and bake for an additional 20 munutes or until chicken is tender.
4 Servings.

PER SERVING:

Calories	211.4	Protein	31.57g
Total Fat	2.85g	Carbohydrate	14.92g
Saturated Fat	2.52g	Cholesterol	40.00mg
Sodium	520.5mg	Fiber	0.58g

ORANGE CHICKEN

1. 4 (5 oz.) Chicken Breasts (boneless, skinless)
2. 1 Cup Sugar Free Orange Soda
3. 1/4 Cup Low Sodium Soy Sauce
4. 4-6 Green Onions (finely chopped)

Combine soda and soy sauce. Marinate chicken breasts in mixture at least 8 hours or overnight in refrigerator. Place chicken and marinade in large baking dish. Sprinkle with onions and bake at 350 degrees for 1 hour. Baste occassionally. 4 Servings.

PER SERVING:

Calories	164.0	Protein	32.21g
Total Fat	2.54g	Carbohydrate	2.47g
Saturated Fat	2.51g	Cholesterol	40.00mg
Sodium	945.4mg	Fiber	0.46g

CROCK POT CHICKEN

1. 4 (5 oz.) Chicken Breasts (boneless, skinless)
2. 1 Small Cabbage (quartered)
3. 1 Pound Package of Mini Carrots
4. 2 Large Cans (14 1/2 oz.) Mexican Flavored
   Stewed Tomatoes

Place above ingredients in crock pot. Cover and cook on low 6-7 hours. 4 Servings.

PER SERVING:

Calories	266.0	Protein	34.34g
Total Fat	2.81g	Carbohydrate	26.77g
Saturated Fat	2.55g	Cholesterol	40.00mg
Sodium	970.8mg	Fiber	4.21g

MEXICAN CHICKEN

1. 4 (5 oz.) Chicken Breasts (boneless, skinless)
2. 1 Jar (16 oz.) Mild Thick Chunky Salsa
3. 1 Can (2 1/4 oz.) Sliced Black Olives (drained)
4. 1/2 Teaspoon Finely Chopped Garlic

Beat chicken breasts to uniform thickness. Spray nonstick frying pan with olive oil flavored spray. Saute garlic over low heat. Add chicken and over low/medium heat cook until golden, turning once. Add salsa and cover. Continue to cook over low/medium heat 30-40 minutes. Good served over rice. Top with olives. 4 Servings.

PER SERVING:

Calories	270.6	Protein	47.23
Total Fat	4.21g	Carbohydrate	9.49g
Saturated Fat	2.73g	Cholesterol	60.00mg
Sodium	1279mg	Fiber	0.03g

CRANBERRY CHICKEN

1. 6 (5 oz.) Chicken Breasts (skinless, boneless)
2. 1 Bottle (8 oz.) Fat Free Catalina Salad Dressing
3. 1 Package Dry Onion Soup Mix
4. 1 Can (16 oz.) Whole Cranberry Sauce

Combine Catalina dressing, onion soup and whole cranberry sauce. Pour over chicken breasts. Place in refrigerator and marinate overnight or at least two hours. Remove from marinade, reserving marinade to brush chicken while baking. Bake uncovered for 45 minutes at 350 degrees. 6 Servings.

PER SERVING:

Calories	323.9	Protein	31.91g
Total Fat	3.00g	Carbohydrate	40.53g
Saturated Fat	2.59g	Cholesterol	40.33mg
Sodium	1248mg	Fiber	1.43g

MANDARIN CHICKEN BREASTS

1. 4 (5 oz.) Chicken Breasts (skinless, boneless)
2. 1 Envelope Dry Onion Soup Mix
3. 1 Can (8 oz.) Pineapple Chunks (undrained)
4. 1 Can (11 oz.) Mandarin Orange (undrained)

On stovetop over low heat brown chicken breasts in non-stick skillet. Combine onion soup mix, pineapple chunks and mandarin oranges. Pour over chicken breasts. Simmer for 30-40 minutes or until chicken is done. 4 Servings.

PER SERVING:

Calories	263.7	Protein	32.82g
Total Fat	3.08g	Carbohydrate	26.47g
Saturated Fat	2.63g	Cholesterol	40.49mg
Sodium	1232mg	Fiber	2.20g

ITALIAN CHICKEN

1. 4 (5 oz.) Chicken Breasts (skinless, boneless)
2. 1 Cup Fat Free Italian Dressing
3. 1 Teaspoon Lemon Pepper
4. 1/8 Teaspoon Salt

Combine Italian dressing, lemon pepper and salt. Pour over chicken breasts and marinate for 2 hours or more in refrigerator. Remove chicken from marinade and bake uncovered at 350 degrees for 45 minutes. Broil for last 5 minutes. 4 Servings.

PER SERVING:

Calories	174.00	Protein	31.00g
Total Fat	2.50g	Carbohydrate	4.00g
Saturated Fat	2.50g	Cholesterol	40.00mg
Sodium	1333mg	Fiber	0g

CHICKEN AND RICE

1. 8 (5 oz.) Chicken (boneless, skinless)
2. 2 Boxes (6.2 oz.) Uncle Ben's Wild Rice Mix
3. 1 Can (4 oz.) Sliced Mushrooms
4. 1 Can (11 oz.) Mandarin Oranges

Place rice in bottom of roaster with cover. Sprinkle with 1 of the seasoning packets in rice. Lay chicken over rice. Pour mushrooms and oranges with juice over chicken. Sprinkle top with second seasoning packet. Add water, according to package directions, to cover rice. Cover and bake at 350 degrees, about 2 hours. Remove cover for last 20 minutes. 8 Servings.

PER SERVING:

Calories	252.2	Protein	33.86
Total Fat	2.73g	Carbohydrate	22.95g
Saturated Fat	2.51g	Cholesterol	40.00mg
Sodium	639.6mg	Fiber	1.06g

HONEY BAKED CHICKEN BREASTS

1. 4 (5 oz.) Chicken Breasts (skinless, boneless)
2. 1/2 Cup Honey
3. 1/2 Cup Dijon Mustard
4. 1 Cup Seasoned Bread Crumbs

Combine honey and mustard. Dip chicken in honey mixture and roll in bread crumbs. Place on foil covered baking pan. Bake at 400 degrees for 30 minutes. Spoon remaining honey mixture over chicken breasts and continue to bake for 10-15 minutes. 4 Servings.

PER SERVING:

Calories	345.0	Protein	34.21g
Total Fat	3.07g	Carbohydrate	38.33g
Saturated Fat	2.66g	Cholesterol	40.44mg
Sodium	1644mg	Fiber	0.06g

TASTY CHICKEN

1. 4 (5 oz.) Chicken Breasts (skinless, boneless)
2. 1/3 Cup Tomato Juice
3. 1/2 Teaspoon Garlic Powder
4. 1/2 Teaspoon Oregano

Pound chicken with meat tenderizer mallet until uniform thickness. Roll chicken breasts in tomato juice. Place chicken on foil in baking dish and sprinkle with garlic and oregano mixture. Bake uncovered at 350 degrees for 45 minutes. 4 Servings.

PER SERVING:

Calories	155.2	Protein	31.23g
Total Fat	2.53g	Carbohydrate	1.23g
Saturated Fat	2.51g	Cholesterol	40.00mg
Sodium	412.8mg	Fiber	0.12g

BAKED CHIMICHANGAS

1. 8 (6-inch) Fat Free Flour Tortillas
2. 1 1/2 Cups Cooked and Cubed Chicken
3. 2 Ounces Grated Low Fat Cheese
4. 3/4 Cup Thick and Chunky Salsa

Mix chicken, cheese and salsa. Warm tortillas until pliable in 400 degree oven or 5 seconds each in microwave. Dampen one side of tortilla with water and place wet side down. Spoon on chicken mixture. Fold to hold in filling. Spray baking dish with non-stick cooking spray. Lay chimichangas, seam side down, on baking dish. Bake for 15 minutes. 4 Servings.

PER SERVING:

Calories	317.5	Protein	30.68g
Total Fat	4.35g	Carbohydrate	35.43g
Saturated Fat	2.02g	Cholesterol	56.22mg
Sodium	844.2mg	Fiber	0g

ROLLED CHICKEN AND ASPARAGUS

1. 4 (5 oz.) Chicken Breasts (boneless, skinless)
2. 30 Asparagus Spears (tough ends removed)
3. 2 Tablespoons Lemon Juice
4. 6 Green Onions (chopped)

Cut chicken breasts into 8 or 10 strips, each about 1-inch by 5-inches long. Wrap each strip in a corkscrew fashion around 2 or 3 asparagus spears. Fasten with toothpicks. Place in a covered baking dish that has been sprayed with a non-stick cooking spray. Sprinkle with lemon juice and onions. Cover and bake at 350 degrees for 30 minutes. Remove toothpicks. Serve hot or refrigerate until chilled and serve cold. 4 Servings.

PER SERVING:

Calories	180.8	Protein	33.73g
Total Fat	2.74g	Carbohydrate	6.47g
Saturated Fat	2.55g	Cholesterol	40.00mg
Sodium	344.2mg	Fiber	2.63g

YOGURT CUMIN CHICKEN

1. 4 (5 oz.) Chicken Breasts (boneless, skinless)
2. 1/3 Cup Nonfat Yogurt
3. 1/4 Cup Apricot Jam
4. 1 Teaspoon Cumin

Place chicken in baking dish that has been sprayed with cooking spray. Bake, uncovered, for 30 minutes at 350 degrees. Mix yogurt, apricot jam, and cumin. Spoon over chicken. Bake for 15 minutes or until chicken is no longer pink and sauce is heated. 4 Servings.

PER SERVING:

Calories	209.6	Protein	32.36g
Total Fat	2.54g	Carbohydrate	14.57g
Saturated Fat	2.50g	Cholesterol	40.47mg
Sodium	373.0mg	Fiber	0.24g

SAUSAGE AND SAUERKRAUT

1. 1 Pound Smoked Turkey Sausage
2. 1 Jar (32 oz.) Sauerkraut (drained)
3. 2 Cups Unpeeled Potatoes (thinly sliced)
4. 1/2 Cup Onion (thinly sliced)

Place sauerkraut in large casserole. Top with onions and potatoes. Cut sausage into serving pieces (about 10) and place on top of potatoes and onions. Cover and cook at 350 degrees for 1 hour or until potatoes are tender. 8 Servings.

PER SERVING:

Calories	142.0	Protein	11.24
Total Fat	5.07g	Carbohydrate	13.67g
Saturated Fat	1.27g	Cholesterol	36.45mg
Sodium	1236mg	Fiber	3.61g

MARY'S WHITE CHILI

1. 1 Pound Ground Turkey
2. 2 Cans (15 oz.) Great Northern Beans
3. 1 Can (16 oz.) White Hominy
4. 1 Package Lawry's Chili Seasoning

Brown turkey in non-stick skillet. Drain any fat from pan. Add undrained beans and hominy. Combine chili seasoning with the 1/2 cup water called for in package and add to turkey chili. Bring to a boil, reduce heat and simmer for 20 minutes and until thoroughly heated. 8 Servings.

PER SERVING:

Calories	264.4	Protein	19.19g
Total Fat	5.82g	Carbohydrate	33.77g
Saturated Fat	1.47g	Cholesterol	44.79mg
Sodium	463.0mg	Fiber	6.63g

Lowfat Recipe Samples From Volume I and II:

WORCHESTER CHICKEN (Volume I)

1. 6 (5 oz.) Chicken Breasts (skinned, boned)
2. 1/4 Cup Worchestershire Sauce
3. 1/2 Cup Fat Free Margarine
4. 2 Tablespoons Lemon Pepper

Place chicken in large casserole sprayed with cooking spray. Spread margarine on each piece of chicken. Sprinkle with lemon pepper and worchestershire sauce. Bake, uncovered, at 350 degrees for 1 hour. 6 Servings.

PER SERVING:

Calories	160.0	Protein	31.00g
Total Fat	2.50g	Carbohydrate	0.67g
Saturated Fat	2.50g	Cholesterol	40.00mg
Sodium	824.3mg	Fiber	0g

CONFETTI CHICKEN (Volume II)

1. 1 1/2 Cups Chicken (cooked and cubed)
2. 2 Cans (14 1/2 oz.) Seasoned Tomatoes/Onions
3. 1 Green Pepper (chopped)
4. 2 Cups Rice (cooked)

In skillet, combine first three ingredients and season to taste. Simmer for 15 minutes. Serve over rice. 4 Servings.

PER SERVING:

Calories	279.6	Protein	19.40g
Total Fat	2.32g	Carbohydrate	43.86g
Saturated Fat	0.65g	Cholesterol	40.43mg
Sodium	619.3mg	Fiber	0.33g

If you are trying to reduce the fat in your diet, always remove the skin of poultry before you cook it; choose oven-frying over deep fat or skillet frying; choose chicken breasts over legs or thighs - the white meat contains less fat than dark meat.

FISH

SWEET MUSTARD FISH

1. 1 Pound Cod
2. 1/2 Cup Thick and Chunky Salsa
3. 2 Tablespoons Honey
4. 2 Tablespoons Dijon Mustard

Arrange fish in baking casserole that has been sprayed with nonstick cooking spray. Bake at 450 degrees, uncovered, for 4-6 minutes. Drain any liquid. Combine remaining ingredients and spoon over fish. Return to oven for 2 minutes to heat sauce. 4 Servings.

PER SERVING:

Calories	157.4	Protein	24.23g
Total Fat	0.76g	Carbohydrates	10.65g
Saturated Fat	0.15g	Cholesterol	53.76mg
Sodium	441.7mg	Fiber	0.02g

SCALLOP KABOBS

1. 1 Pound Fresh Sea Scallops
2. 2 Large Green Peppers (cut 1-inch squares)
3. 1 Pint Cherry Tomatoes
4. 1 (8 oz.) Bottle Fat Free Italian Salad Dressing

Combine all ingredients in shallow dish. Cover and marinate at least 3 hours, stirring occasionally. On skewers, alternate scallops, green peppers, and cherry tomatoes. Place on broiler rack and brush with remaining dressing. Broil 4-inches from heat 5 minutes, turn once and baste with dressing. 4 Servings.

PER SERVING:

Calories	150.3	Protein	20.08g
Total Fat	1.21g	Carbohydrates	12.78g
Saturated Fat	0.14g	Cholesterol	37.42mg
Sodium	984.8mg	Fiber	1.60g

BAKED COD VINAIGRETTE

1. 1 Lb. Cod Fillets
2. 3 Tablespoons Fat Free Vinaigrette Dressing
3. Paprika
4. 1 Tablespoon Minced Chives

Arrange fillets in shallow baking dish and brush with salad dressing. Sprinkle with paprika and chives. Bake, uncovered at 450 degrees for 10-12 minutes or until fillets flake with a fork. 4 Servings.

PER SERVING:

Calories	98.84	Protein	20.22g
Total Fat	0.77g	Carbohydrates	1.16g
Saturated Fat	0.15g	Cholesterol	48.76mg
Sodium	211.3mg	Fiber	0.02g

TEXAS BOILED BEER SHRIMP

1. 2 Lbs. Unshelled Large Raw Shrimp (deheaded)
2. 2 (12-oz.) Cans Lite Beer
3. 2 Tablespoons Crab Boil Seasoning

In large pot, bring beer to boil with seasoning. Stir in shrimp and cover. Return to boil and simmer for 5 minutes. Turn heat off and leave shrimp in hot beer for a few more minutes. Drain shrimp and serve immediately. Serve with lemon wedges and cocktail sauce.
4 Servings.

PER SERVING:

Calories	240.4	Protein	46.06g
Total Fat	3.92g	Carbohydrates	2.06g
Saturated Fat	0.74g	Cholesterol	344.7g
Sodium	335.7mg	Fiber	0g

SPICY SHRIMP

1. 1 Lb. Large Raw Shrimp (peeled and cleaned)
2. 1/2 Cup Fat Free Margarine
3. 1/2 Lb. Fresh Mushrooms (sliced)
4. Chili Seasoning

Melt 1/4 cup of margarine in skillet and add shrimp. Saute shrimp just until tender and pink (about 5 minutes). Stir in remaining margarine and mushrooms and cook 5 minutes more. Sprinkle shrimp with chili seasoning (use like you would use pepper). Good served over rice. 4 Servings.

PER SERVING:

Calories	240.4	Protein	46.06g
Total Fat	3.92g	Carbohydrates	2.06g
Saturated Fat	0.74g	Cholesterol	344.7mg
Sodium	335.7mg	Fiber	0g

BROILED SHRIMP

1. 1 Pound Shrimp (cleaned, peeled)
2. 2 Tablespoons Olive Oil
3. 2 Tablespoons Minced Garlic
4. 4 Teaspoons Chopped Parsley

Combine oilive oil, garlic and parsley. Roll the shrimp in mixture and broil until pink (about five minutes). 4 Servings.

PER SERVING:

Calories	190.8	Protein	23.52g
Total Fat	8.75g	Carbohydrates	3.43g
Saturated Fat	1.29g	Cholesterol	172.4mg
Sodium	169.6mg	Fiber	0.15g

ORANGE ROUGHY WITH RED PEPPERS

1. 1 Lb. Orange Roughy
2. 1 Small Onion (cut into thin slices)
3. 2 Medium Red Bell Peppers ((cut into strips)
4. 1 Teaspoon Dried Thyme Leaves

Cut fillets into 4 serving pieces. Spray heated skillet with nonstick cooking spray. Layer onion and pepper in skillet. Sprinkle with 1/2 teaspoon thyme. Place fish over onion/ pepper layer. Sprinkle with remaining thyme. Cover and cook over low heat 15 minutes. Uncover and cook until fish flakes easily with fork (about 10 minutes). 4 Servings.

PER SERVING:

Calories	161.4	Protein	17.26g
Total Fat	8.07g	Carbohydrates	4.33g
Saturated Fat	0.17g	Cholesterol	22.68mg
Sodium	72.97mg	Fiber	1.17g

COMPANY HALIBUT STEAKS

1. 4 (4 oz.) Halibut Steaks
2. 1/2 Cup Apricot Preserves
3. 2 Tablespoons White Vinegar
4. 1/2 Teaspoon Dried Tarragon Leaves

Spray broiler pan rack with nonstick cooking spray. Place fish steaks on rack and broil 4-inches from heat for 4 minutes. Turn fish and broil 4 minutes longer. Mix remaining ingredients and spoon onto fish. Broil 1 minute longer or until fish flakes easily with fork. 4 Servings.

PER SERVING:

Calories	222.6	Protein	23.88g
Total Fat	2.68g	Carbohydrates	26.20g
Saturated Fat	0.37g	Cholesterol	36.29mg
Sodium	77.31mg	Fiber	0.48g

TARRAGON FISH

1. 1 Pound Fish Fillets
2. 1/2 Cup Plain Nonfat Yogurt
3. 1 Teaspoon Dried Tarragon
4. 1 Ounce Grated Reduced Fat Mozzarella Cheese

Arrange fish in baking casserole that has been sprayed
with nonstick cooking spray. Bake at 450 degrees,
uncovered, for 4-5 minutes. Drain any liquid. Mix
remaining ingredients and spread over fish. Bake 2
minutes or until cheese is melted. 4 Servings.

PER SERVING:

Calories	129.2	Protein	24.26g
Total Fat	1.74g	Carbohydrates	2.70g
Saturated Fat	0.09g	Cholesterol	46.83mg
Sodium	135.8mg	Fiber	0.03g

BROILED SALMON STEAKS

1. 2 (8 oz.) Salmon Steaks (halved)
2. Nonfat Butter Spray
3. 1 Teaspoon Dried Marjoram
4. Freshly Ground Pepper

Spray salmon with nonfat butter flavored spray. Sprinkle
with 1/2 marjoram and pepper. Spray broiler rack with
nonstick spray. Broil steaks 4-inches from heat source
until first side is lightly browned (5 to 8 minutes). Spray,
turn, and sprinkle with remaining half of marjoram and
pepper. Broil 5-8 minutes longer or until fish flakes easily
with fork. 4 Servings.

PER SERVING:

Calories	204.5	Protein	22.77g
Total Fat	11.85g	Carbohydrates	0.09g
Saturated Fat	2.84g	Cholesterol	74.84mg
Sodium	53.41mg	Fiber	0.03g

CRUNCHY BAKED FISH

1. 1 Pound Fish Fillets
2. 1/3 Cup Finely Crushed Cheez-It Crackers
3. 1 Teaspoon Parsley Flakes
4. 1/2 Cup Lowfat Catalina Salad Dressing

Preheat oven 400 degrees. Mix crackers and parsley. Brush both sides of fish with Catalina Dressing. Coat one side of fish with cracker mixture. Place fish, cracker side up, on cookie sheet sprayed with nonstick cooking spray. Bake, uncovered, until fish flakes easily with fork, 10-15 minutes. 4 Servings.

PER SERVING:

Calories	137.8	Protein	20.33g
Total Fat	3.26g	Carbohydrates	6.89g
Saturated Fat	0.15g	Cholesterol	48.76mg
Sodium	318.2mg	Fiber	0g

EASY CHEESY FISH FILLETS

1. 1 Pound Fish Fillets
2. 1 Onion (thinly sliced)
3. 1/4 Cup Fat Free Mayonnaise
4. 1/4 Cup Grated Fat Free Flavored Cheese Product

Place fillets in a single layer in baking casserole. Spread with mayonnaise and sprinkle with cheese. Top with onions. Cover and bake at 450 degrees for 10 minutes. Uncover and bake 4-6 minutes more, until browned. 4 Servings.

PER SERVING:

Calories	122.7	Protein	22.68g
Total Fat	0.79g	Carbohydrates	4.98g
Saturated Fat	015g	Cholesterol	48.76mg
Sodium	251.8mg	Fiber	0.36g

TANGY APRICOT FISH

1. 1 Pound Fish Fillets
2. 1/3 Cup Nonfat Yogurt
3. 3 Tablespoons Apricot Jam
4. 1 Tablespoon Lemon Juice

Arrange fish in baking casserole that has been sprayed with nonstick cooking spray. Bake at 450 degrees, uncovered, for 4-5 minutes. Drain any liquid. Mix remaining ingredients and pour over fish. Bake for 2 minutes longer to heat sauce. 4 Servings.

PER SERVING:

Calories	137.7	Protein	21.24g
Total Fat	0.74g	Carbohydrates	11.06
Saturated Fat	0.09g	Cholesterol	42.37mg
Sodium	97.69mg	Fiber	0.20g

LEMON BUTTER DILL FISH

1. 1 Pound Fish Fillets
2. 3/4 Cup Fat Free Lemon Butter Dill Sauce for Seafood
3. 1/4 Cup Red Pepper (thinly sliced)
4. 1 Tablespoon Parmesan Cheese

Brush both sides of fish with 1/2 cup dill sauce. Arrange fish in baking casserole that has been sprayed with nonstick cooking spray. Place red pepper slices on top of fish. Drizzle rest of dill sauce over tops of fish and peppers. Sprinkle with parmesan. Bake, uncovered, at 350 degrees for 20 minutes or until fish flakes easily with a fork. 4 Servings.

PER SERVING:

Calories	140.4	Protein	21.57g
Total Fat	3.95g	Carbohydrates	4.45g
Saturated Fat	0.39g	Cholesterol	49.74mg
Sodium	593.6mg	Fiber	0.13g

Lowfat Recipe Samples From Volume I and II:

BARBEQUED TROUT (Volume 1)

1. 4 Trout
2. 4 Tablespoons Minced Onion
3. 1 Cup Fat Free Barbecued Sauce
4. Salt and Pepper

Place onion, BBQ sauce in body cavity of trout. Salt and pepper to taste. Wrap trout individually in foil and bake at 350 degrees for 20 minutes. 4 Servings.

PER SERVING:

Calories	223.0	Protein	19.10g
Total Fat	4.11g	Carbohydrates	23.14g
Saturated Fat	1.15g	Cholesterol	94.12mg
Sodium	341.2mg	Fiber	0.18g

BAKED ORANGE ROUGHY (Volume II)

1. 1 Pound Orange Roughy Fillets
2. 1/4 Cup Lemon Juice
3. 1/2 Teaspoon Tarragon Leaves
4. 2 Teaspoons Dried Mustard

Place fillets in large casserole that has been sprayed with nonstick cooking spray. Squeeze lemon juice over fillets. Sprinkle dried mustard and tarragon leaves over fish. Bake at 400 degrees for 25 minutes. 4 Servings.

PER SERVING:

Calories	146.7	Protein	16.73g
Total Fat	7.94g	Carbohydrates	1.31g
Saturated Fat	0.15g	Cholesterol	22.68mg
Sodium	71.59mg	Fiber	0.06g

SPANISH FISH (Volume II)

1. 1 (1 Lb.) Fish (Snapper, Redfish)
2. 1 Bell Pepper (chopped)
3. 1 Red Onion (chopped)
4. 1 Can (14 1/2 oz.) Seasoned Tomatoes

Line shallow pan with foil leaving ample amount hanging over the edges. Pour 1/3 of the tomatoes onto the foil. Place fish over tomatoes. Sprinkle the bell pepper and onion over the fish. Pour remaining tomatoes over fish and loosely close up foil. Bake at 350 degrees for 20 minutes per pound or until fish is flakey. 4 Servings.

PER SERVING:

Calories	167.8	Protein	24.89g
Total Fat	1.65g	Carbohydrates	12.52g
Saturated Fat	0.34g	Cholesterol	41.96mg
Sodium	366.9mg	Fiber	1.39g

Most fish are excellent sources of low-fat protein and have fewer calories than other meats. The most important rule to remember when cooking seafood is to not overcook it. Also when buying fresh fish, refrigerate it in the coldest section of your refrigerator. If you don't plan to use it within a day or two, freeze it.

PORK

SAGE SEASONED PORK CHOPS

1. 4 (1/2-inch) Pork Loin Chops (trim fat from chops)
2. 1/2 Teaspoon Dried Sage
3. 1 Small Onion (sliced and separated into rings)
4. 2 Apples (cored and cut into thin wedges)

Rub sage onto both sides of chops. Place chops in a large skillet sprayed with nonstick cooking spray. Cook chops for 5 minutes on one side. Turn chops and add onion and apples. Cook for 7 minutes more or until chops are thoroughly cooked. 4 Servings.

PER SERVING:

Calories	287.0	Protein	37.87g
Total Fat	8.88g	Carbohydrate	12.35g
Saturated Fat	3.02g	Cholesterol	107.2mg
Sodium	112.9mg	Fiber	2.25g

BEST PORK TENDERLOIN

1. 1 1/2 Pounds Pork Tenderloin
2. 1 Teaspoon Black Pepper
3. 1 Teaspoon Rosemary Leaves
4. 1 Cup Barbecue Sauce

Rub tenderloin with pepper and rosemary leaves. Bake at 350 degrees for 1 -1/2 hours. Slice and serve with warmed barbecue sauce. 6 Servings.

PER SERVING:

Calories	185.8	Protein	24.09g
Total Fat	6.90g	Carbohydrate	5.34g
Saturated Fat	2.24g	Cholesterol	74.99mg
Sodium	395.9mg	Fiber	0.50g

HONEY MUSTARD PORK TENDERLOIN

1. 2 (1 1/2 Lb.) Pork Tenderloins
2. 1/2 Cup Honey
3. 2 Teaspoons Prepared Mustard
4. 1/4 Cup Brown Sugar

Mix honey, mustard and brown sugar. Spread over pork tenderloins and let marinate at least 2 hours in refrigerator. Roast at 350 degrees for 1 hour. 12 Servings.

PER SERVING:

Calories	182.2	Protein	19.41g
Total Fat	5.12g	Carbohydrate	14.46g
Saturated Fat	1.76g	Cholesterol	62.12mg
Sodium	56.51mg	Fiber	0.03g

LEMON AND GARLIC ROAST PORK

1. 1 (3 Lb.) Lean Boneless Pork Loin Roast
2. 3/4 Teaspoon Grated Lemon Rind
3. 3 Garlic Cloves (minced)
4. 1 Can Low-Salt Chicken Broth

Trim fat from pork. Combine lemon rind and garlic and rub evenly over pork. Place pork in a casserole dish and add broth. Bake at 400 degrees for 30 minutes. Turn pork over and bake an additional 35 minutes. Discard broth and serve. 12 Servings.

PER SERVING:

Calories	166.1	Protein	24.60g
Total Fat	6.51g	Carbohydrate	0.48g
Saturated Fat	2.20g	Cholesterol	66.64mg
Sodium	68.60mg	Fiber	0.02g

DEVILED PORK ROAST

1. 1 (3 Lb.) Lean Pork Loin Roast
2. 2 Tablespoons Dijon Mustard
3. 1 Teaspoon Ground Thyme
4. Fresh Ground Pepper to Taste

Spread pork roast with thin coating of mustard. Sprinkle with thyme and pepper. Roast, uncovered, at 375 degrees for 1 1/2 hours. 12 Servings.

PER SERVING:

Calories	164.3	Protein	24.21g
Total Fat	6.40g	Carbohydrate	0.07g
Saturated Fat	2.21g	Cholesterol	66.64mg
Sodium	118.6mg	Fiber	0.02g

HEALTHY STYLE QUESADILLAS

1. 4 Fat Free Flour Tortillas
2. 4 Teaspoons Prepared Honey Mustard
3. 1 Cup Fat Free Cheese (shredded)
4. 4 Slices 98% Fat Free Ham

Spread each tortilla with 1 teaspoon mustard. Sprinkle with cheese and top with 1 ham slice. Fold tortilla in half. In large nonstick skillet over medium-high heat, place one or two filled tortillas. Cook until cheese melts, about 1 minute per side. Serve with salsa if desired. 4 Servings.

PER SERVING:

Calories	199.0	Protein	26.49g
Total Fat	1.42g	Carbohydrate	18.42g
Saturated Fat	0.46g	Cholesterol	13.32mg
Sodium	627.4mg	Fiber	0g

BAKED PORK TENDERLOIN

1. 1 (1 1/2 Lb.) Lean Pork Tenderloin
2. Butter Flavored Non-Fat Spray
3. 2 Cups Canned Fat Free Chicken Broth
4. 1 Can (4 oz.) Mushroom Stems and Pieces

Brown meat in generous coating of butter flavored nonfat spray. Remove from skillet and place in casserole. Add a little flour to drippings and add chicken broth and mushrooms. Stir until heated and mixed. Pour over pork and bake at 350 degrees for 1 hour. 6 Servings.

PER SERVING:

Calories	144.2	Protein	24.20g
Total Fat	3.93g	Carbohydrate	1.27g
Saturated Fat	1.35g	Cholesterol	73.86mg
Sodium	384.5mg	Fiber	0.45g

PORK TENDERLOIN SUPREME

1. 2 (1 1/2 Lbs.) Lean Pork Tenderloin
2. 1 Can Tomato Soup
3. 1 Package Onion Soup Mix
4. 2 Tablespoons Worcestershire Sauce

Place tenderloins in center of large sheet of tin foil. Mix remaining ingredients and spread over meat. Seal securely in foil. Place in shallow pan and bake for 2 hours at 325 degrees. Cut meat into 1-inch slices. Pour soup-gravy over slices of meat. 12 Servings.

PER SERVING:

Calories	139.7	Protein	20.49g
Total Fat	3.78g	Carbohydrate	5.13g
Saturated Fat	1.22g	Cholesterol	61.30mg
Sodium	463.2mg	Fiber	0.36g

MARINATED PORK TENDERLOIN

1. 1 (1 1/2 Lb.) Pork Tenderloin Roast
2. 1 Tablespoon Sherry
3. 2 Tablespoons Low Sodium Soy Sauce
4. 2 Tablespoons Brown Sugar

Combine sherry, soy sauce and brown sugar. Rub over roast and marinate overnight in refrigerator. Roast at 300 degrees until tender 1 1/2 hours. 6 Servings.

PER SERVING:

Calories	172.1	Protein	23.65g
Total Fat	6.15g	Carbohydrate	3.55g
Saturated Fat	2.13g	Cholesterol	74.99mg
Sodium	400.7mg	Fiber	0g

PINEAPPLE PORK

1. 2 Pounds Lean Pork Shoulder Meat
    (cut in 1-inch cubes)
2. 1 Can (14 oz.) Pineapple Chunks
    (drained, reserving liquid)
3. 1/4 Cup Vinegar
4. 1 Teaspoon Ginger

Combine above ingredients and simmer in nonstick skillet for 1 hour. Add pineapple liquid if needed. Chill, skim off fat and reheat. Good served over rice. 8 Servings.

PER SERVING:

Calories	195.9	Protein	22.19g
Total Fat	8.11g	Carbohydrate	7.16g
Saturated Fat	2.81g	Cholesterol	75.98mg
Sodium	90.71mg	Fiber	0.47g

HAM IN WINE SAUCE

1. 1 1/2 Pound Lean Cooked Sliced Ham
2. 1 Cup Currant Jelly
3. 1 Cup Red Cooking Wine
4. 4 Tablespoons Sugar

Combine jelly, wine and sugar in saucepan. Cook over medium heat until mixture comes to a boil, stirring constantly. Continue to boil to a thick syrup. Serve over heated slices of ham. 8 Servings.

PER SERVING:

Calories	252.7	Protein	16.80g
Total Fat	4.30g	Carbohydrate	33.08g
Saturated Fat	1.38g	Cholesterol	39.97mg
Sodium	1233mg	Fiber	0.44g

RAISIN SPICED HAM STEAK

1. 1 Pound Lean Ready-to-Eat Ham Steak
2. 1/2 Teaspoon Pumpkin Pie Spice
3. 1/2 Cup Unsweetened Pineapple Juice
4. 2 Tablespoons (1 oz.) Raisins

Brown and heat ham steak in a nonstick skillet sprayed with cooking spray. Remove steak to heated platter. Combine remaining ingredients and cook over high heat, stirring constantly, until mixture is reduced to a few tablespoons. Pour over ham steak. 4 Servings.

PER SERVING:

Calories	212.2	Protein	22.46g
Total Fat	5.77g	Carbohydrate	17.19g
Saturated Fat	1.85g	Cholesterol	53.30mg
Sodium	1622mg	Fiber	0.49g

HAWAIIAN PORK CHOPS

1. 4 Lean Pork Loin Chops (1/2-inch thick)
2. 1 Can (8 oz.) Pineapple Slices In Own Juice
3. 2 Tablespoons Brown Sugar
4. 1/2 Teaspoon Ground Nutmeg

Drain and reserve juice from canned pineapple. Place pork chops in baking dish that is lightly sprayed with cooking spray. Mix 3 tablespoons of the reserved pineapple juice with brown sugar and nutmeg. Spoon half of the mixture over the pork chops. Top with pineapple slices and spoon remaining mixture over pineapple. Cover and bake 30 minutes at 350 degrees. Uncover and bake 20 minutes longer, spoon sauce over chops occasionally. 4 Servings.

PER SERVING:

Calories	305.9	Protein	37.86g
Total Fat	10.37g	Carbohydrate	13.45g
Saturated Fat	3.60g	Cholesterol	93.55mg
Sodium	78.92mg	Fiber	0.45g

SAVORY BROILED PORK CHOPS

1. 4 (5 oz.) Lean Pork Loin Chops (3/4-inch thick)
2. 3 Tablespoons Dijon Mustard
3. 1 Teaspoon Dried Thyme
4. Freshly Ground Pepper

Spread half the mustard evenly over chops and sprinkle with half the thyme. Sprinkle with pepper. Broil 6 inches from heat 10 to 12 minutes. Turn chops and spread with remaining mustard and remaining thyme. Sprinkle with pepper. Broil second side until browned, around 10-12 minutes. 4 Servings.

PER SERVING:

Calories	223.4	Protein	31.37g
Total Fat	8.55g	Carbohydrate	0.22g
Saturated Fat	2.94g	Cholesterol	77.96mg
Sodium	334.0mg	Fiber	0.07g

ORANGE PORK CHOPS

1. 4 Lean Pork Rib Chops
2. 1/3 Cup Light Orange Marmalade
3. 2 Tablespoons Dijon Mustard
4. 4 Bunches Green Onions

In small saucepan mix marmalade and mustard and stir over medium heat until marmalade is melted. Set aside. Place chops on broiler rack. Broil chops about 4 inches from heat for 6 minutes; turn and broil for 2 more minutes. Spoon half of the glaze over chops and broil 5 minutes more or until chops are no longer pink. In separate skillet sprayed with nonstick cooking spray, stir-fry the onions 2 minutes or until crisp-tender. Stir in remaining glaze and heat thoroughly. Serve over pork chops. 4 Servings.

PER SERVING:

Calories	278.3	Protein	38.49g
Total Fat	10.31g	Carbohydrate	4.00g
Saturated Fat	3.54g	Cholesterol	93.55mg
Sodium	264.2mg	Fiber	1.25g

CHINESE BARBECUED PORK

1. 1 1/2 Pounds Boneless Pork Tenderloin
2. 1/2 Cup Chinese Barbecue Sauce
3. Bottled Hot Mustard

Marinate pork in barbecue sauce overnight in refrigerator. Remove from marinade and place pork in roasting pan. Roast pork for 1 1/2 hours at 325 degrees or until meat juices run clear. Slice 1/8-inch thick and refrigerate until ready to serve. Serve pork with hot mustard. 6 Servings.

PER SERVING:

Calories	260.1	Protein	24.67g
Total Fat	8.70g	Carbohydrate	18.54g
Saturated Fat	2.54g	Cholesterol	70.19mg
Sodium	811.4mg	Fiber	0g

HAM AND POTATOES O'BRIEN CASSEROLE

1. 4 Slices Fat Free Ham Luncheon Meat (cubed)
2. 1 (24 oz.) Package Ore Ida Frozen Potatoes O'Brien
    (thawed)
3. 1 (8 oz.) Package Fat Free Cream Cheese
    (room temperature)
4. 1 (4.5 oz.) Can Chopped Green Chilies

Preheat oven to 400 degrees. Combine cream cheese and
green chilies. Pour over potatoes and ham and stir until
well mixed. Place in 1 quart oven proof casserole that
has been sprayed with cooking spray. Bake 40 minutes.
Pepper to taste. 4 Servings.

PER SERVING:

Calories	142.8	Protein	0.00g
Total Fat	0.94g	Carbohydrates	23.83g
Saturated Fat	0.31g	Cholesterol	8.90mg
Sodium	563.6mg	Fiber	3.26g

MINTED LAMB PATTIES

1. 1 Lb. Lean Ground Lamb
2. 1/4 Cup Dry Bread Crumbs
3. 2 Tablespoons Dried Mint
4. 1 Teaspoon Lemon Pepper

Mix all ingredients thoroughly and shape into 4 patties.
Spray broiler pan with nonstick cooking spray. Broil
patties about 3 inches from heat for about 8-10 minutes
or until no longer pink inside, turning once. 4 Servings.

PER SERVING:

Calories	183.9	Protein	24.37g
Total Fat	7.03g	Carbohydrate	3.99g
Saturated Fat	2.48g	Cholesterol	74.84mg
Sodium	204.5mg	Fiber	0.23g

LAMB WITH YOGURT-MINT SAUCE

1. 4 Lamb Loin Chops (fat trimmed)
2. 1/3 Cup Plain Nonfat Yogurt
3. 1/4 Cup Mint Jelly
4. 2 Tablespoons Jalopeno Jelly

Blend yogurt, mint and jalopeno jellies and save for sauce. Spray broiler pan with nonstick cooking spray. Broil lamb chops 3-inches from heat for 12-14 minutes, turning chops after 6 minutes. Serve with sauce. 4 Servings.

PER SERVING:

Calories	352.0	Protein	34.96g
Total Fat	15.73g	Carbohydrate	16.81g
Saturated Fat	5.63g	Cholesterol	112.6mg
Sodium	140.4mg	Fiber	0g

Lowfat Recipe Samples From Volume 1 and II:

ROAST PORK IN MARINADE (Volume I)

1. 4 Pounds Lean Pork Roast
2. 1 Can (15 oz.) Tomatoes (chopped)
3. 1/4 Cup White Vinegar
4. 1/4 Cup Water

Place roast in roasting pan. Mix and pour the remaining ingredients over roast. Best marinated overnight. Cover and bake at 350 degrees for 4 hours. 10 Servings.

PER SERVING:

Calories	268.8	Protein	39.28g
Total Fat	10.37g	Carbohydrate	2.18g
Saturated Fat	3.55g	Cholesterol	107.0mg
Sodium	163.7mg	Fiber	0.43g

GRILLED PORK CHOPS (Volume II)

1. 4 (1-inch thick) Pork Chops
2. 1/4 Teaspoon Salt
3. 3/4 Teaspoon Lemon Pepper
4. 1/2 Teaspoon Dried Whole Oregano Leaves

Mix salt, lemon pepper and oregano. Coat pork chops.
Grill over low to medium hot heat for 25 minutes or until
chops are no longer pink. Turn once. 4 Servings.

PER SERVING:

Calories	253.4	Protein	37.61g
Total Fat	10.22g	Carbohydrate	0g
Saturated Fat	3.52g	Cholesterol	93.55mg
Sodium	281.9mg	Fiber	0g

THE OTHER WHITE MEAT: Pork is a white
meat, not only in terms of color, but more
importantly because it is a lean meat that is low in
fat and calories. America's pork producers have
reduced the average fat content of pork by 31
percent and lowered average calories by 14 percent
according to USDA figures. There are eight pork
cuts that are lower than skinless chicken thigh in
terms of fat and cholesterol content. The tenderloin
is the leanest cut of pork.

BEEF

BROILED FLANK STEAK

1. 1 1/2 Lbs. Lean Beef Flank Steak
2. 3/4 Cup Dry Red Wine or Cooking Wine
3. 1 1/2 Teaspoons Lemon Pepper
4. 1 Teaspoon Garlic

Combine wine, garlic and lemon pepper; pour over steak. Cover and marinate in refrigerator overnight. Coat broiler rack with cooking spray and place flank steak on rack. Let flank steak return to room temperature. Broil 3-4 inches from heat for 5-7 minutes on each side. Slice steak across grain into thin slices to serve. 8 Servings.

PER 3 OZ. SERVING:

Calories	155.6	Protein	17.64g
Total Fat	6.42g	Carbohydrate	0.84g
Saturated Fat	2.77g	Cholesterol	43.09mg
Sodium	144.7mg	Fiber	0g

FLANK STEAK AND SPINACH PINWHEELS

1. 1 1/2 Pounds Lean Beef Flank Steak
2. 1 Package (10 oz.) Frozen Spinach (thawed, drained)
3. 1/4 Cup Grated Parmesan Cheese
4. 1/4 Cup Fat Free Sour Cream

Cut shallow diagonal cuts on one side of steak and pound to 3/8-inch thickness. Combine spinach, sour cream and cheese and spread on cut-side of steak. Starting at narrow end, roll up steak and secure with toothpicks at 1-inch intervals. Cut into 1-inch slices (leaving picks in steak) and place pinwheels on broiler rack sprayed with cooking spray. Broil 6-inches from heat 7 minutes on each side. Remove picks and serve. 8 Servings.

PER 3 OZ. SERVING:

Calories	156.1	Protein	20.18
Total Fat	7.15g	Carbohydrate	2.24g
Saturated Fat	3.22g	Cholesterol	44.49mg
Sodium	142.9mg	Fiber	1.06g

SOUTHWESTERN BEEF COMBO

1. 1/2 Pound Lean Ground Beef
2. 1 Small Onion (chopped)
3. 3 Cups Frozen Potatoes O'Brien (thawed)
4. 1 Cup Salsa

Brown ground beef and onion in large skillet. Pour off any drippings. Stir in potatoes and cook over medium-high heat for 5 minutes, stirring occasionally. Stir in salsa and continue to cook 10 minutes longer. 6 Servings.

PER SERVING:

Calories	178.5	Protein	12.87g
Total Fat	7.85g	Carbohydrate	13.84g
Saturated Fat	3.15g	Cholesterol	35.09mg
Sodium	307.1mg	Fiber	1.58g

SAVORY CHUCK STEAKS

1. 4 (6 oz.) Boneless Lean Beef Chuck Eye Steaks
2. 1/4 Cup Steak Sauce
3. 2 Tablespoons Brown Sugar
4. 3 Tablespoons Fresh Lime Juice

Combine steak sauce, brown sugar and lime juice, reserving 2 tablespoons of this marinade. Place beef in plastic bag and add remaining marinade, turning to coat. Close bag securely and marinate for 10 minutes. Pour off marinade and grill steaks for 14-20 minutes for rare to medium done. Brush with reserved 2 tablespoons of marinade during last 2 minutes of cooking. 4 Servings.

PER SERVING:

Calories	342.8	Protein	49.36
Total Fat	9.71g	Carbohydrate	11.45g
Saturated Fat	3.52g	Cholesterol	117.4mg
Sodium	257.3mg	Fiber	0.05g

CREOLE PEPPER STEAK

1. 1 Pound Beef Top Round Steak (cut 1-inch thick)
2. 2 Cloves Garlic (crushed)
3. 1 Teaspoon Dried Thyme
4. 1 Teaspoon Red Pepper

Combine garlic, thyme and red pepper. Press evenly into both sides of steak. Grill 12-14 minutes for rare to medium, turning once. Cut steak diagonally into thin slices to serve. 4 Servings.

PER SERVING:

Calories	197.3	Protein	24.77g
Total Fat	9.94g	Carbohydrate	0.50g
Saturated Fat	4.13g	Cholesterol	68.04mg
Sodium	56.96mg	Fiber	0.03g

ORANGE PEPPER STEAKS

1. 4 (4 oz.) Beef Tenderloin Steaks (cut 1-inch thick)
2. 1/2 Cup Sugar Free Orange Marmalade
3. 4 Teaspoons Cider Vinegar
4. 1/2 Teaspoon Ground Ginger

Combine marmalade, vinegar and ginger. Place steaks on rack in broiler pan and brush top of steaks with half of marmalade mixture. Broil 3-inches from heat for 10-15 minutes, turning once. Brush with remaining marmalade mixture after turning. 4 Servings.

PER SERVING:

Calories	265.0	Protein	24.41g
Total Fat	12.17g	Carbohydrate	12.30g
Saturated Fat	4.86g	Cholesterol	66.90mg
Sodium	66.95mg	Fiber	0g

CHUCK ROAST STEAKS

1. 3 Pounds Boneless Chuck Roast (trim fat)
2. 1 Teaspoon Pepper
3. 1 Teaspoon Garlic Powder
4. 1 Teaspoon Onion Powder

Combine pepper, garlic powder and onion powder. Sprinkle roast with mixture. Place on rack in broiler pan. Broil 5 inches from the heat 5 minutes per side. Remove from broiler, cool until it can be cut easily. Slice roast crosswise about 1-inch thick. Place slices under broiler until lightly brown, turn and brown other side. 12 Servings.

PER SERVING:

Calories	266.1	Protein	37.37g
Total Fat	11.67g	Carbohydrate	0.42g
Saturated Fat	4.43g	Cholesterol	114.1mg
Sodium	74.77mg	Fiber	0.06g

FLANK STEAK

1. 1 1/2 Pounds Lean Beef Flank Steak
2. 1/4 Cup Fat Free Margarine (melted)
3. 1 Teaspoon Garlic Powder
4. 1/2 Cup Dry Sherry

Combine sherry, margarine and garlic. Pour half mixture over beef and broil 3-inches from heat for 5-7 minutes. Turn, pour remaining mixture over beef and broil for 3 more minutes. Slice diagonally and serve. 8 Servings.

PER 3 OZ. SERVING:

Calories	152.5	Protein	17.36g
Total Fat	6.33g	Carbohydrate	0.84g
Saturated Fat	2.73g	Cholesterol	42.52mg
Sodium	108.5mg	Fiber	0g

FLANK STEAK JOY

1. 1 1/2 Pounds Lean Flank Steak
2. 2 Tablespoons Soy Sauce
3. 1 Tablespoon Sherry
4. 1 Teaspoon Honey

Combine soy sauce, sherry and honey. Pour over steak. Marinate several hours in refrigerator. Line a shallow pan with foil and place steak on foil. Broil about 10 minutes on each side. 8 Servings.

PER 3 OZ. SERVING:

Calories	138.3	Protein	17.51g
Total Fat	6.33g	Carbohydrate	1.18g
Satuated Fat	2.73g	Cholesterol	42.52mg
Sodium	319.5mg	Fiber	0g

BEEF GOULASH

1. 2 Pounds Lean Stew Beef
2. 1 Large Onion (chopped)
3. 1 Can (11.5 oz.) V8 Vegetable Juice
4. 1/2 Teaspoon Pepper

Brown meat and onions in non-stick skillet. Add V8 vegetable juice and pepper. Cover and simmer 1 1/2 hours. Good served with noodles. 8 Servings.

PER SERVING:

Calories	277.9	Protein	37.92g
Total Fat	11.35g	Carbohydrate	3.64g
Saturated Fat	4.30g	Cholesterol	114.5mg
Sodium	209.6mg	Fiber	0.36g

COMPANY BEEF TENDERLOIN

1. 6 (4 oz.) Beef Tenderloin Steaks
2. 8 Ounces Fresh Mushrooms (sliced)
3. 1 Large Clove Garlic (minced)
4. 1 Cup Cooking Sherry

In large nonstick skillet sprayed with cooking spray, saute mushrooms and garlic for 4 minutes. Add sherry and cook until liquid is reduced. Stir frequently, set aside and keep warm. Broil tenderloin steaks for 5 minutes on each side. Arrange on platter and pour heated sherried mushroom sauce over steaks. 6 Servings.

PER SERVING:

Calories	289.3	Protein	32.93g
Total Fat	10.68g	Carbohydrate	3.48g
Saturated Fat	4.14g	Cholesterol	95.25mg
Sodium	76.45mg	Fiber	0.47g

VEAL MARSALA

1. 1 Pound Veal (thinly sliced)
2. 1/4 Cup Flour
3. 2 Tablespoons Fat Free Margarine
4. 1/2 Cup Marsala Wine

Lightly dredge sliced veal in flour. Brown veal in margarine in a heavy skillet. Add Marsala wine. Cover pan and simmer over low heat for 5 minutes. 4 Servings.

PER SERVING:

Calories	176.1	Protein	23.77g
Total Fat	3.01g	Carbohydrate	6.33g
Saturated Fat	0.90g	Cholesterol	89.58mg
Sodium	138.2mg	Fiber	0.21g

GROUND MEAT AND BEAN CASSEROLE

1. 1/2 Pound Extra Lean Ground Beef
2. 1/2 Cup Onion (chopped)
3. 2 Cans (16 oz.) Baked Beans
4. 1/4 Cup Catsup

Brown ground meat in skillet. Add onion and cook until
tender. Add beans and catsup and heat thoroughly.
6 Servings.

PER SERVING:

Calories	185.9	Protein	10.64g
Total Fat	8.23g	Carbohydrate	19.42g
Saturated Fat	3.24g	Cholesterol	28.41mg
Sodium	446.1mg	Fiber	4.16g

Lowfat Recipe Samples From Volume I and II:

SHERRIED BEEF (Volume I)

1. 2 Pounds Lean Beef (cubed in 1 1/2-inch cubes)
2. 2 Cans Cream of Mushroom Soup - Healthy Request
3. 1/2 Cup Cooking Sherry
4. 1/2 Package Dry Onion Soup Mix

Mix all ingredients in casserole and bake covered at 250
degrees for 3 hours. Good served with rice. 8 Servings.

PER SERVING:

Calories	224.4	Protein	25.77g
Total Fat	7.41g	Carbohydrate	9.12g
Saturated Fat	2.06g	Cholesterol	64.73mg
Sodium	1003mg	Fiber	0.37g

BEEF ROAST (Volume II)

1. 3 Pound Eye of Round Roast
2. Cracked Peppercorns

Preheat oven to 500 degrees. Roll roast in peppercorns. Place in baking dish, then in preheated oven. Bake 5-6 minutes per pound. Turn oven off and leave roast in oven for 2 more hours. DO NOT OPEN OVEN DURING THIS TIME. Bake uncovered for medium done roast. 8 Servings.

PER SERVING:

Calories	224.5	Protein	37.00g
Total Fat	7.31g	Carbohydrate	0g
Saturated Fat	2.52g	Cholesterol	91.85mg
Sodium	90.15mg	Fiber	0g

Trimming all external fat from lean beef reduces the total fat content by an average of over 50 percent. When looking for the leanest cuts of beef, remember this rule of thumb: Look for the words "round" or "loin" - beef eye round, top round, round tip, top sirloin, top loin and tenderloin. If you are trying to reduce the fat content in your diet, be aware and reduce serving sizes - especially with beef and other meats.

DESSERTS

ORANGE ANGEL FOOD CAKE

1. 1 Package Angel Food Cake Mix
2. 3/4 Cup Frozen Orange Juice Concentrate (thawed)
3. 1 Container (8 oz.) Lite Cool Whip
4. 1/2 Cup Plain Lowfat Yogurt

Prepare angel food cake as directed on package, but pour 1/3 cup of thawed orange juice into a 2-cup measure and add enough water for the mixture to equal the amount of water called for in package directions. Bake according to directions. Cool. Combine Cool Whip, yogurt and remaining orange juice concentrate. Spoon orange sauce on individual slices of cake. 12 Servings.

PER SERVING:

Calories	206.8	Protein	5.42g
Total Fat	0.93g	Carbohydrates	44.26g
Saturated Fat	0.68g	Cholesterol	0.62mg
Sodium	113.9mg	Fiber	0.14g

CHOCOLATE ANGEL CAKE

1. 1 Package Angel Food Cake Mix
2. 1/3 Cup Unsweetened Cocoa Powder

Prepare cake mix according to package directions. Sift cocoa powder and add to cake mix. Then continue as directed on package. 12 Servings.

PER SERVING:

Calories	164.6	Protein	4.97g
Total Fat	.36g	Carbohydrates	36.75g
Saturated Fat	.19g	Cholesterol	0mg
Sodium	108.6mg	Fiber	.73g

ANGEL CAKE

1. 1 Package White Angel Food Cake Mix
2. 1 Cup Skim Milk
3. 1 Package (1 oz.) Milk Chocolate Sugar Free Instant Pudding Mix
4. 2 Cups (16 oz.) Lite Cool Whip

Prepare cake according to package directions for tube pan. Split cake horizontally to make 2 layers. Beat milk and pudding mix until well blended. Fold in Cool Whip. Frost layers and top of cake. Refrigerate at least 1 hour before serving. 12 Servings.

PER SERVING:

Calories	202.8	Protein	5.43g
Total Fat	1.52g	Carbohydrates	41.50g
Saturated Fat	1.37g	Cholesterol	0.37mg
Sodium	151.3mg	Fiber	0g

CHOCOLATE GLAZED ANGEL FOOD CAKE

1. 3 Cups Sifted Powdered Sugar
2. 1/4 Cup Unsweetened Cocoa
3. 1/4 Cup plus 1 1/2 Tablespoon Hot Water
4. 1 Prepared Angel Food Cake

In bowl combine first three ingredients and stir until smooth. Drizzle over angel food cake. 12 Servings.

PER SERVING:

Calories	287.3	Protein	4.87g
Total Fat	0.32g	Carbohydrates	68.17g
Saturated Fat	0.15g	Cholesterol	0mg
Sodium	108.8mg	Fiber	0.55g

PEACH CRISP

1. 2 Cans (16 oz.) Sliced Peaches (drained)
2. 1/4 Cup Sugar
3. 2 Teaspoons Cornstarch
4. 3/4 Cup Lowfat Granola (without raisins)

In small bowl combine peaches, sugar and cornstarch. Spoon peach mixture into 4 custard cups coated with cooking spray. Place cups on a baking sheet and sprinkle granola over tops of each custard cup. Bake at 400 degrees uncovered for 25 minutes or until thoroughly heated and tops are crisp. 4 Servings.

PER SERVING:

Calories	167.7	Protein	2.41g
Total Fat	1.15g	Carbohydrates	39.55g
Saturated Fat	0.19g	Cholesterol	0mg
Sodium	48.64mg	Fiber	1.99g

SUGARED ANGEL FOOD CAKE

1. 1 1/2 Cups Sifted Powdered Sugar
2. 2 Tablespoons Skim Milk
3. 1/2 Teaspoon Vanilla
4. 1 Prepared Angel Food Cake

In small bowl combine first three ingredients. Drizzle over angel food cake layers. 12 Servings.

PER SERVING:

Calories	222.4	Protein	4.63g
Total Fat	0.08g	Carbohydrates	51.54g
Saturated Fat	0.02g	Cholesterol	0.05mg
Sodium	109.6mg	Fiber	0g

LEMON ANGEL FOOD CAKE

1. 1 1/2 Cups Sifted Powdered Sugar
2. 2 Tablespoons Lemon Juice plus 1 Tablespoon Hot Water
3. 1 Teaspoon Vanilla Extract
4. 1 Prepared Angel Food Cake

In small bowl combine first three ingredients. Drizzle over angel food cake layers. 12 Servings.

PER SERVING:

Calories	222.2	Protein	4.55g
Total Fat	0.08g	Carbohydrates	51.63g
Saturated Fat	0.01g	Cholesterol	0mg
Sodium	108.4mg	Fiber	0.01g

SHORTCAKE DROP BISCUITS

1. 1 Cup Self-Rising Flour
2. 3 Tablespoons Diet Margarine (room temperature)
3. 7 Tablespoons Skim Milk
4. I Teaspoon Vanilla Extract

Combine above ingredients until batter is blended. Drop batter by tablespoonfuls onto a nonstick cookie sheet which has been sprayed with cooking spray. Bake about 10 minutes at 450 degrees or until golden brown. This can be served with crushed berries, peaches or other fresh fruit. 8 Servings.

PER SERVING:

Calories	78.30	Protein	1.99g
Total Fat	2.24g	Carbohydrates	12.15g
Saturated Fat	0.38g	Cholesterol	0.24mg
Sodium	252.5mg	Fiber	0.51g

OATMEAL MACAROONS

1. 2 Egg Whites
2. 1/3 Cup Maple Syrup
3. 1 Cup Rolled Oats
4. 1/2 Cup Grated Coconut

Beat egg whites until stiff. Combine syrup and oats in separate bowl and mix until well blended. Add coconut. Fold in beaten whites. Drop by teaspoonful (walnut size) onto lightly greased cookie sheet. Bake at 350 degrees for 15 minutes. Makes 30 Servings.

PER SERVING:

Calories	27.72	Protein	0.71g
Total Fat	0.75g	Carbohydrates	4.94g
Saturated Fat	0.51g	Cholesterol	0mg
Sodium	8.05mg	Fiber	0.34g

CHOCOLATE GINGER SPICE SQUARES

1. 1 Package Dry Gingerbread Mix
2. 2 Packages (3.4 oz.) Fat Free Chocolate Pudding Mix (not instant)
3. 1/4 Teaspoon Ground Cinammon
4. 1 Cup Water

Combine above ingredients in a mixing bowl. Beat 1 minute on medium speed. Pour into 13x9x2-inch nonstick cake pan and bake at 350 degrees for 35 minutes. Allow to cool slightly or chill. Cut into squares. 32 Servings.

PER SERVING:

Calories	74.15	Protein	0.88g
Total Fat	1.95g	Carbohydrates	13.84g
Saturated Fat	0.50g	Cholesterol	0mg
Sodium	154.9mg	Fiber	0.04g

GINGERALE BAKED APPLES

1. 4 Baking Apples
2. 4 Tablespoons Golden Raisins
3. 4 Teaspoons Brown Sugar
4. 1/2 Cup Gingerale

Core apples without cutting through the bottom. Stand apples in baking dish just large enough to hold them. Place 1 tablespoon raisins and 1 teaspoon brown sugar in center of each apple. Pour in the gingerale. Bake at 350 degrees for 45 minutes, basting frequently, until apples are tender but not mushy. Serve warm or chilled. 4 Servings.

PER SERVING:

Calories	122.8	Protein	0.55g
Total Fat	0.54g	Carbohydrates	31.88g
Saturated Fat	0.09g	Cholesterol	0mg
Sodium	2.85mg	Fiber	4.09g

BANANAS ROSANNA

1. 1 Pint Fresh Strawberries
2. 1 Can (6 oz.) Orange Juice (concentrate, thawed, undiluted)
3. 3 Large Ripe Bananas (sliced)
4. 1 Carton (8 oz.) Fat Free Cool Whip

Wash, hull and cut up strawberries. Combine them in blender with undiluted orange juice concentrate and blend until smooth. Alternate banana slices with strawberry-orange sauce. Top with Cool Whip. Serve chilled. 8 Servings.

PER SERVING:

Calories	140.1	Protein	1.30g
Total Fat	0.40g	Carbohydrates	32.24g
Saturated Fat	0.09g	Cholesterol	0mg
Sodium	17.35mg	Fiber	2.10g

PINEAPPLE COCONUT SHERBET

1. 2 Cans (8 oz.) Unsweetened Crushed Pineapple
    in Own Juice (drained)
2. 2 Cups Nonfat Vanilla Yogurt
3. 1/2 Cup Unsweetened Shredded Coconut
4. 2 Tablespoons Honey

Combine all ingredients and stir well. Pour into shallow pan and freeze until partially set. Transfer to a bowl and beat 4 minutes. Pour into a container with cover and freeze until solid. Soften at room temperature for about 15 minutes before serving. 8 Servings.

PER SERVING:

Calories	116.3	Protein	2.93g
Total Fat	2.06g	Carbohydrates	22.22g
Saturated Fat	1.83g	Cholesterol	1.25mg
Sodium	54.19mg	Fiber	0.65g

CHOCOLATE EXPRESS

1. 6 Tablespoons Chocolate Liqueur
2. 1 Envelope Plain Gelatin
3. 1 1/2 Cups Hot Black Coffee
4. 2 Cup Fat Free Chocolate Ice Cream

Combine liqueur and gelatin in blender container. Wait for 1 minute, then add hot coffee. Cover and blend until gelatin granules are dissolved. Add ice cream and blend until smooth. Pour into 4 custard cups and chill until set. 4 Servings.

PER SERVING:

Calories	215.2	Protein	4.49g
Total Fat	0.08g	Carbohydrates	36.56g
Saturated Fat	0g	Cholesterol	0mg
Sodium	77.21mg	Fiber	0g

SHERRIED FRUIT

1. 1 Package (12 oz.) Mixed Berries
2. 2 Cups Cantaloupe Balls
3. 1 Can (8 oz.) Pineapple Chunks
4. 1/4 Cup Cooking Sherry

Combine fruit in large bowl. Add sherry and toss lightly. Cover and chill at least 2 hours or overnight. Serve chilled. 6 Servings.

PER SERVING:

Calories	75.04	Protein	0.87g
Total Fat	0.33g	Carbohydrates	18.56g
Saturated Fat	0g	Cholesterol	0g
Sodium	21.96mg	Fiber	2.76g

FROZEN BLUEBERRY-BANANA DESSERT

1. 2 Cups Nonfat Vanilla Frozen Yogurt
2. 2 Bananas
3. 1 Cup Frozen Blueberries
4. 1/4 Cup Frozen Concentrated Apple Juice

Thaw frozen yogurt just enough to cut into chunks. In blender puree yogurt and remaining ingredients. Serve immediately or freeze for 15 minutes before serving. 6 Servings.

PER SERVING:

Calories	141.2	Protein	3.23g
Total Fat	0.39g	Carbohydrates	32.25g
Saturated Fat	0.08g	Cholesterol	0mg
Sodium	33.64mg	Fiber	1.66g

GINGERSNAP-BAKED PEARS

1. 1 Can (16 oz.) Unsweetened Pear Halves (drained)
2. 12 Lowfat Gingersnaps (finely crushed)
3. 2 Tablespoons Sugar
4. 2 Tablespoons Lowfat Margarine (melted)

Arrange pears, cut side up, in a 9-inch cakepan. Combine remaining ingredients. Spread over pears. Bake at 300 degrees for 20 minutes. Serve warm. 4 Servings.

PER SERVING:

Calories	151.7	Protein	0.91g
Total Fat	4.65g	Carbohydrates	26.25g
Saturated Fat	0.83g	Cholesterol	0mg
Sodium	224.2mg	Fiber	2.45g

CAPPUCCINO ICE

1. 3 Cups Strong Brewed Coffee
2. 2 Cups Lite Cool Whip (thawed)
3. 2 Tablespoons Sugar
4. 2 Tablespoons Cocoa

Combine all ingredients in blender. Blend at low speed until smooth. Pour into 8-inch square baking pan, cover and freeze until firm. Remove from freezer and let frozen mixture stand at room temperature for 30 minutes. Again spoon into blender and process until smooth. Return to baking pan, cover and freeze until firm. When ready to serve, let stand 5 minutes at room temperature and spoon into serving dishes. 6 servings.

PER SERVING:

Calories	64.81	Protein	0.45g
Total Fat	2.90g	Carbohydrates	8.06g
Saturated Fat	2.81g	Cholesterol	0mg
Sodium	2.74mg	Fiber	0.55g

GRANOLA SUNDAE

1. 1 Cup Lowfat Vanilla Yogurt
2. 1 Cup Lowfat Granola Mix
3. 2 Cups Bananas (sliced)
4. 1 Pint Strawberries (washed, sliced)

Layer yogurt, granola and fruit into four 8-ounce stemmed glasses or bowls. Refrigerate until ready to serve.
4 Servings.

PER SERVING:

Calories	280.8	Protein	6.61g
Total Fat	3.07g	Carbohydrates	62.09g
Saturated Fat	0.47g	Cholesterol	2.50mg
Sodium	91.87mg	Fiber	5.91g

COMPANY PEACH DELIGHT

1. 2 Cans (16 oz.) Lite Peach Halves
2. 4 Tablespoons Fat Free Cream Cheese
3. 6 Tablespoons Brown Sugar
4. 1 Teaspoon Ground Cinnamon

Fill center of peaches with 1 tablespoon cream cheese and place halves together. Combine brown sugar and cinnamon. Roll peaches in brown sugar mixture. Chill until ready to serve. 4 Servings.

PER SERVING:

Calories	133.1	Protein	2.96g
Total Fat	0.06g	Carbohydrates	32.41mg
Saturated Fat	0g	Cholesterol	0mg
Sodium	86.41mg	Fiber	1.80g

STRAWBERRY PINEAPPLE CUPS

1. 3 Ripe Bananas
2. 3 Containers (6 oz.) Yoplait Lowfat Yogurt (any flavor)
3. 1 Package (10 oz.) Frozen Strawberries
   (thawed and undrained)
4. 1 Can (8 oz.) Crushed Pineapple (undrained)

Line 18 medium muffin cups with paper baking cups. In medium bowl, mash bananas with fork. Stir in remaining ingredients and spoon into cups. Freeze at least 3 hours or until firm. Remove from paper cups and let stand 10 minutes before serving. 18 Servings.

PER SERVING:

Calories	44.46	Protein	1.44g
Total Fat	0.11g	Carbohydrates	10.02g
Saturated Fat	0.04g	Cholesterol	0mg
Sodium	15.07mg	Fiber	0.91g

PINEAPPLE MELBA

1. 1 Fresh Pineapple (market sliced, 12 rings)
2. 3 Tablespoon Sugar
3. 1 Can (8 oz.) Sliced Peaches (drained)
4. 1/2 Cup Raspberries

Place pineapple rings on serving plate. Sprinkle with sugar. In blender, blend peaches until smooth. Top pineapple with peach sauce and fresh raspberries. 12 Servings.

PER SERVING:

Calories	40.40	Protein	0.29g
Total Fat	0.21g	Carbohydrates	10.29g
Saturated Fat	0.01g	Cholesterol	0mg
Sodium	0.97mg	Fiber	0.98g

PUMPKIN ICE-CREAM PIE FILLING

1. 1 Can (18 oz.) Pumpkin Pie Mix
2. 1 Pint Fat Free Vanilla Ice Cream
3. 1/2 Cup Brown Sugar
4. 2 Tablespoons Fat Free Margarine

Beat pumpkin pie and ice cream together. Spoon into a prepared light graham cracker crust. Freeze 1 hour. In saucepan heat brown sugar and margarine to boiling. Remove from heat and drizzle over pie. Freeze until firm. Let pie stand at room temperature 15 minutes before serving. 8 Servings.

PIE FILLING PER SERVING:

Calories	151.7	Protein	2.70g
Total Fat	0.08g	Carbohydrates	36.15g
Saturated Fat	0.04g	Cholesterol	0mg
Sodium	188.7mg	Fiber	0g

STRAWBERRY DREAM PIE FILLING

1. 1 Package (10 oz.) Frozen Sweetened Strawberry Halves (defrosted)
2. 1 Package (.3 oz.) Sugar Free Strawberry Jello
3. 1 Container (8 oz.) Fat Free Strawberry Yogurt
4. 2 Cups Fat Free Vanilla Ice Cream (softened)

In mixing bowl, combine strawberry halves, jello and yogurt. Add ice cream and mix until well combined. Pour into a prepared light graham cracker pie crust. Place in freezer for at least 4 hours before serving. Let stand at room temperature for 30 minutes before serving. Makes 8 servings of pie filling.

PIE FILLING PER SERVING:

Calories	212.7	Protein	4.94g
Total Fat	3.05g	Carbohydrates	41.21g
Saturated Fat	1.00g	Cholesterol	0.83mg
Sodium	171.1mg	Fiber	1.67g

CHERRY VANILLA TRIFLE

1. 1 Fat Free Prepared Angel Food Cake
   (torn into bite-size pieces)
2. 2 Containers (8 oz.) Fat Free Cherry Vanilla Yogurt
3. 4 Containers Prepared Jello Fat Free Vanilla
   Pudding Snacks
4. 1 Can (20 oz.) Sweet Cherries (drained)

Combine yogurt and pudding. Beginning with cake pieces, place a layer of cake with a layer of yogurt/pudding mix. Sprinkle with cherries. Repeat, ending with yogurt/pudding mixture. Cover and refrigerate. 10 Servings.

PER SERVING:

Calories	172.3	Protein	5.02g
Total Fat	0.28g	Carbohydrates	38.13g
Saturated Fat	0.04g	Cholesterol	0mg
Sodium	346.4mg	Fiber	0.83g

PINEAPPLE ORANGE FLUFF

1. 1 Package (.3 oz.) Sugar Free Orange Jello
2. 1 Can (15 oz.) Crushed Pineapple (undrained)
3. 2 Cups Buttermilk
4. 1 Container (8 oz.) Fat Free Cool Whip

Heat crushed pineapple and add orange jello. Stir until jello is dissolved. Cool about 15 minutes. Add buttermilk and cool whip. Stir until blended and refrigerate until firm. 10 Servings.

PER SERVING:

Calories	87.12	Protein	2.14g
Total Fat	0.43g	Carbohydrates	16.61g
Saturated Fat	0.27g	Cholesterol	1.72mg
Sodium	90.21mg	Fiber	0.38g

BROWNIE COOKIES

1. 1 Package (18 oz.) Krusteaz Fat Free Fudge
   Brownie Mix
2. 1/3 Cup Water
3. 1/3 Cup Powdered Sugar

Pre-heat oven to 375 degrees. Mix brownie mix with water. Form into 1-inch balls. Dip into powered sugar and place onto non-stick cookie sheet. Bake for 8-10 minutes. 32 Cookies.

PER SERVING:

Calories	64.93	Protein	0.50g
Total Fat	0g	Carbohydrates	15.27g
Saturated Fat	0g	Cholesterol	0mg
Sodium	79.96mg	Fiber	0.50g

TRIPLE RASPBERRY CREAM

1. 1 Package (8 oz.) Fat Free Cream Cheese
   (room temperature)
2. 1 Can (12 oz.) Country Raspberry Frozen
   Concentrate Juice (softened)
3. 10 Raspberry Flavored Fruit Newton Cookies -
   Fat Free (softened)
4. 1 Quart Fat Free, No Sugar Raspberry Ice Cream

Cream cheese until fluffy. Gradually add juice concentrate and beat until well combined. Add softened ice cream and beat. Process cookies until they make a fine crumb. Place 1/2 of ice cream mixture in bottom of 8x8-inch square pan. Sprinkle with cookie crumbs (reserve 2 tablespoons for topping). Place remainder of cream mixture on top of cookie layer. Sprinkle with cookie crumbs. Freeze. 12 Servings.

PER SERVING:

Calories	187.6	Protein	5.34g
Total Fat	0g	Carbohydrates	40.52g
Saturated Fat	0g	Cholesterol	0mg
Sodium	185.6mg	Fiber	0.41g

SNOW TOPPED BROWNIE MOUNDS

1. 1 Package Krusteaz Fat Free Brownie Mix
2. 1/3 Cup Water
3. 45 Minature Marshmallows (about 1/2 cup)

Combine mix and water. It will be very stiff and sticky. When mix is thoroughly moistened, make small 1-inch balls. Place balls in mini muffin pans that have been sprayed with cooking spray. Push one minature marshmallow into each cookie ball. Bake at 350 degrees for 8-10 minutes. Makes 45 cookies.

PER SERVING:

Calories	43.71	Protein	0.36g
Total Fat	0g	Carbohydrates	10.23g
Saturated Fat	0g	Cholesterol	0mg
Sodium	56.52mg	Fiber	0.35g

BANANA CREAM PUDDING

1. 1 Package (.9 oz) Fat Free Sugar Free Jello Banana Cream Pudding Mix
2. 2 1/2 Cup Lowfat Milk
3. 12 Reduced Fat Vanilla Wafers
4. 2 Bananas (sliced)

Mix pudding with milk. Layer 6 cookies, 1 sliced banana and half of pudding. Repeat layers with remaining ingredients ending with pudding. Refrigerate. 6 Servings.

PER SERVING:

Calories	136.9	Protein	4.63g
Total Fat	2.93g	Carbohydrates	24.39g
Saturated Fat	1.36g	Cholesterol	7.29mg
Sodium	318.2mg	Fiber	1.16g

LOWFAT VANILLA FROSTING

1. 1 Carton (16 oz.) Fat Free Vanilla Yogurt
2. 1/2 Cup Confectioners Sugar
3. 1/2 Teaspoon Vanilla

Mix above ingredients until well blended. Refrigerate until chilled. Spread on cake just before serving. Makes 2 Cups.

PER SERVING:

Calories	61.12	Protein	3.25g
Total Fat	0g	Carbohydrates	12.46g
Saturated Fat	0g	Cholesterol	1.25mg
Sodium	40.08mg	Fiber	0g

ORANGE TOPPING

1. 1 Cup Orange Juice
2. 2 Tablespoons Cornstarch
3. 1 Orange (peeled, sectioned)

In saucepan, mix the cornstarch with a small amount of juice. Add remaining juice and stir over medium heat until thickened. Cool slightly. Mix orange slices with juice mixture and pour over cake. Makes topping for 8 servings.

PER SERVING:

Calories	29.06	Protein	0.41g
Total Fat	0.10g	Carbohydrates	6.89g
Saturated Fat	0.01g	Cholesterol	0mg
Sodium	0.49mg	Fiber	0.47g

MERINGUE SHELL

1. 3 Egg Whites (room temperature)
2. 1/2 Cup Sugar

Preheat over to 300 degrees. Lightly grease 9-inch pie pan. Beat egg whites until foamy. Gradually add sugar a tablespoon at a time and continue to beat until moist and stiff peaks form when beater is withdrawn. Spoon into pie pan so that it cover bottom and sides. Bake for 1 hour until light brown. Cool before filling. Good filled with fresh fruit.

PER SERVING:

Calories	70.41	Protein	1.76g
Total Fat	0g	Carbohydrates	16.19g
Saturated Fat	0g	Cholesterol	0mg
Sodium	27.60mg	Fiber	0g

MERINGUE

1. 3 Egg Whites
2. 1/4 Teaspoon Cream of Tartar
3. 1/2 Teaspoon Vanilla Extract
4. 6 Tablespoons Sugar

Beat egg whites with cream of tartar and vanilla until soft peaks form. Gradually add sugar while beating until stiff and glossy. Spread meringue on pie filling, sealing against edge. Bake for 15 minutes or until peaks are golden brown.

PER SERVING:

Calories	54.90	Protein	1.76g
Total Fat	0g	Carbohydrates	12.18g
Saturated Fat	0g	Cholesterol	0mg
Sodium	27.56mg	Fiber	0g

INDEX

Savory Baked Lemon
Chicken, 70
Sausage and Sauerkraut, 78
Tarragon Chicken, 68
Tasty Chicken, 76
Worchestershire Chicken, 79
Yogurt Cumin Chicken, 78

RICE

Sesame Rice, 59
Sherried Brown Rice Pilaf, 60
Veggie Rice, 60

SALADS

Apple Coleslaw, 29
Apple Salad With Feta
Cheese, 29
Beet and Onion Salad, 30
Bell Pepper Salad, 36
Broccoli Salad, 30
Carrot Raisin Celery Salad, 31
Cucumber Salad, 32
Cucumber Strawberry Salad, 32
Fruit and Spinach Salad, 38
Fruit Salad, 33
Green Bean and Baby Corn, 34
Hearts of Palm Salad, 35
Hearty Spinach and Mushroom
Salad, 36
Italian Tomato Cheese
Salad, 40
Luncheon Tuna Salad, 41
Marinated Cauliflower
Salad, 31
Marinated Vegetable Salad, 42
Medley of Fruit, 34
Romaine Strawberry Salad, 40
Snow Pea Salad, 35
Spinach Chicken Salad, 39
Spinach With Sprouts, 38

Sweet and Sour Cucumber
Salad, 33
Sweet Potato Salad, 39
Sunshine Salad, 37
Tangy Spinach Salad, 37
Turkey Salad, 41

SPREADS

Fruited Cheese Spread, 18
Pimiento Cheese Spread, 19
Pimiento Cream Spread, 18
Spanish Olive Spread, 17
Tropical Cheese Spread, 19

SQUASH

Candied Acorn Squash, 61
Carrots and Zucchini, 49
Skillet Squash, 61
Squash Casserole, 64
Zucchini Squash, 63

VEGETABLES

Asparagus With
Sesame Seeds, 45
Baked Sweet Potatoes, 58
Braised Celery, 50
Candied Acorn Squash, 61
Carrot Casserole, 49
Carrots and Zucchini, 49
Cottage Cheese Stuffed Baked
Potatoes, 56
Cottaged Sweet Potatoes, 58
Dijon Broccoli, 46
Garlic and Herb
Cheese Rice, 59
Garlic Green Beans, 52
Ginger Carrots, 48
Gingered Sweet Potatoes, 57
Green Beans With Dill, 52

MORE OF THE FOUR INGREDIENT COOKBOOK

More Recipes Using Only Four Ingredients!!

E & CALE

See reverse side for Free Offer and then use this form to order additional copies for your family and friends.

THE FOUR INGREDIENT COOKBOOK

Over 200 Recipes Using Four Ingredients!!

COFFEE & CALE

LOW FAT & LIGHT FOUR INGREDIENT COOKBOOK

More Recipes Using Only Four Ingredients!!

COFFEE & CALE

Makes a wonderful gift for Birthdays, Anniversaries, Special Occasions or Christmas and Holiday giving.

Emily & Linda's Cookbook Offer

P.O. Box 2121, Kerrville, Texas 78029-2121
or Call 1-800-757-0838

Please send copy(s) of Emily & Linda's Four Ingredient Cookbook (Vol. I, II, or III) @ $9.95 plus $2.95 shipping and handling. Total $12.90 per book. Texas residents please add $1 tax (Texas total $13.90).

#_____ Copies of Vol. I - *The Four Ingredient Cookbook*

#_____ Copies of Vol. II - *More of the Four Ingredient Cookbook*

#_____ Copies of Vol. III - *Low Fat and Light Four Ingredient Cookbook*

Total number of books_____ @$12.90 (TX. $13.90) = $_____.__

❏ Enlosed is a check for the above amount.

❏ Charge the above amount to my Visa ❏   or Mastercard ❏

Card No._____exp. date___/__

Please name issuing bank_____

* ORDER TWO OR MORE BOOKS AND WE'LL SEND YOU AN EXTRA BOOK
FOR FREE

SHIPPING INFORMATION

NAME_____
PLEASE PRINT

ADDRESS_____APT. #_____

CITY_____

STATE_____ZIP CODE_____

DAY TIME PHONE_____
(MUST HAVE FOR CREDIT CARD ORDERS)